Advance Praise for *Patchwork*

"Lena Cantrell McNicholas has written a book from her heart, for the hearts of us all. Her clear, sharp images bring us to the place, the time, and the people of her beloved Southwest Virginia. She has woven a tapestry, or better yet in the terms of her heritage, a quilt—piecing the memories, giving us a sense of time and place that will never come again. The contrast between that simplicity and beauty of her old home place and the stark, ugly, modern replacements beats true for many of us gone home to a place that can never be again, except in memory. *Patchwork* is a book for today that carries those precious pieces of yesterdays, a book to pass down to the inheritors of tomorrows."

—Elizabeth Doyle Solomon, author of *Seasons*, award-winning poet and founder of the weekly *Central Virginia Leader* newspaper.

■ ■ ■

"These poems, essays and stories are vivid 'slices of time,' mostly of the author's childhood in the mountains of far Southwest Virginia. As her grandfather pointed out, Lena was 'always goin' over yonder somewheres' to places as distant as Europe and Mexico and Venezuela, but her heart never wandered far from the scenes of her early life. The people who populated those rooms and landscapes—her family, her classmates, and the boy who bought her pie at the Pie Supper in 1948—speak to us in this collection of wistful, sad, and joyful memories."

—Jeanne Shannon, author of *Stars Scattered Like Seeds*.

■ ■ ■

"I was recently invited to a reading of Lena McNicholas' poetry and stories. Although I have known Lena for years, I was unprepared for the funny, sensitive and absolutely loveable presentation. She is a true original—a sophisticated writer of very common things. Her writing is as enjoyable as a spring day in the mountains."

—Spero McConnell, DPA, retired, Miami-Dade Public Schools and Florida International University.

■ ■ ■

Patchwork

Best Wishes,
Lena Cantrell McNicholas

Lena Cantrell McNicholas

Patchwork

Pieces of Appalachia

An Appalachian Memoir in poems, stories and essays

■ ■ ■

Lena Cantrell McNicholas

■ ■ ■

MARINER
PUBLISHING

BUENA VISTA, VIRGINIA

1   3   5   7   9   10   8   6   4   2

Library of Congress Control Number: 2010928274
Patchwork: Pieces of Appalachia
Lena Cantrell McNicholas

p. cm.
1. Biographical memoirs 2. Biographical poetry 3. Pound (Va.)
4. Appalachian Mountains—History, Local
5. Folk music—Appalachian Region

I. McNicholas, Lena Cantrell, 1936– II. Title.

ISBN 13: 978-0-9841128-6-9 (softcover : alk. paper)

ISBN 10: 0-9841128-6-3

Cover Art: *Mountain Mural* Lois Bartlett Tracy 1901-2008
Cover Art Photography: Tim Cox
Cover and Book Design: Emilie Davis

Mariner Publishing
A division of
Mariner Media, Inc.
131 West 21st St.
Buena Vista, VA 24416
Tel: 540-264-0021
www.marinermedia.com

Printed in the United States of America

This book is printed on acid-free paper meeting the
requirements of the American Standard for Permanence
of Paper for Printed Library Materials.

The Compass Rose and Pen are trademarks of Mariner Media, Inc.

For Mother and Dad

Tottie Baker Cantrell
c 1956

Fitzhugh Lee Cantrell
1954

APPALACHIAN HYMN

"Precious memories, how they linger
How they ever flood my soul.
In the stillness of the midnight
Precious, sacred scenes unfold"

— AUTHOR UNKNOWN

TABLE OF CONTENTS

■ Acknowledgments ■

I suppose the obvious place to begin is at the beginning with Dad and Mother and the family they created. Dad, Fitzhugh Lee Cantrell, was the first "women's libber" I ever met, even before there was a name for the cause. He treated his daughters with great respect and planned their educations with the same enthusiasm and passion as those of his sons. This was not the norm in the time and place we were raised, but there was never a doubt in my mind that he thought I was capable and talented, and he encouraged me to be myself and not to fear the new and unknown.

Mother, Tottie Baker Cantrell, was a lady, and I knew this at an early age. She worked hard and endlessly to raise five children with high standards of grammar and etiquette. She passed on a love of beauty in fabric, a fine seam, sentimental poems, reading, and the joy of singing. She took pride in canned bounty, and special Sunday dinners that ended with towering cakes and pies. Her faith was unwavering, and her prayers a constant in our lives.

The Pound is a small mountain town in the farthest reaches of southwest Virginia. This town—along with recollections of family, childhood friends, and teachers—has a deep place in my heart. My memories of these are as much a part of my life as breathing and I have carried them with me across the world and back.

The writing of the enclosed pieces began more than twenty years ago at a very troubled time of my life. The sudden deaths of my brother Robert, and husband George, prompted my move from Texas back to Southwest Virginia. Shortly after the move, my brother David's unexpected death almost paralyzed me emotionally, but all systems were needed for Mother's care as she entered the destructive maze called Alzheimer's disease.

My therapy came in buying and restoring a "wreck of an historical house," Litchfield Hall, built circa 1869. I became an innkeeper, and that will be another story.

Fortune and luck seemed to lead me to the right people when my needs were greatest, and once again I found them in Abingdon's Appalachian Poets and

Writers. Dr. Sam Miller encouraged me to keep on writing, and the editor of the *Abingdon Virginian*, Robert Weisfeld, said of my first piece, "that's good Lena, send it to me and I will publish it." Lou Crabtree, now deceased, was a poet laureate, and a friend who inspired me beyond expression. I felt content and wrote sporadically, won a few prizes, published a little, and attended more workshops. The town and people gave me a safe, historically inspiring and visually comforting place to write, heal, and sing again with exuberance. Thank you.

Other dear friends in Abingdon who encouraged and assisted me as I struggled to find my way were Bill Kittrell, Vicki Marsh, Pat Jessee, Spero McConnell, Charlotte Brillhart, and the late Joan Horsch. I will never forget my special friend, Joan Horsch, who gave me gentle critique and friendship.

I could write an essay on Hindman Settlement School, a unique place for writers to gather and *Appalachian Heritage*, a literary quarterly. Both honor the work of writers, past and present, who are steady, and devoted to the task and calling of keeping alive the Appalachian voice. They gently lead the novices and pay homage to the well-known in honoring our past, present, and future. I have been privileged to work with some of the best at Hindman and attend additional workshops as they travel and spread the word. Lee Smith, Ron Rash, Silas House, Sharon McCrumb, Fred Chappell, Wendell Berry, Michael McFee, Lisa Alther, Pamela Duncan and Adriana Trigiani are but of few of the many. Thank you.

As with most of my life, I keep on moving, never knowing what the next journey will bring. Family circumstances influenced me to move again; the death of my brother-in-law James Roberson, Mickey's further progression into Alzheimer's, and his eventual need for institutional care. It would be easier if my remaining siblings and I were living in the same town. I joined my sister, Frances, in Charlottesville and soon brought my brother, Mickey, here.

I was fearful at finding a writing community that would be receptive to my Appalachian stories and poems. Elizabeth Solomon invited me to join her poetry group, which led me to the Blue Ridge Writers Club where I met Gary Kessler. Gary read some of my work and encouraged me to continue and submit to competitions for publication in the *Blue Ridge Anthology*. Some pieces won prizes and some were published. I sporadically attended a poetry group in Scottsville led by Sharron Singelton. This group educated and encouraged me further. Writer House offered a place to read and learn from more experienced writers, but I was still hampered by a lack of the computer skills necessary to keep up with the fast pace the writing and publishing world was taking.

I often wanted to scrap the whole thing and focus on other interests, and when my seventeen-year-old Toshiba laptop crashed, I was positive this was the end. Frustration accompanied every writing session until my niece, Lisa Roberson, came to the rescue—along with Christian of Top Notch Computers—and gently led me through learning my way through the new computer maze. Creativity took a back seat.

A prayer was answered by the appearance of Robert "Rob" Douglas, who patiently helped me edit and make the work presentable for submission. He came to me through Christ Episcopal Church's priest, Paul Walker, and I am eternally grateful.

If I have omitted any Charlottesville friends who have offered encouragement or assistance, please accept my thanks at this time.

I was truly blessed at the 2009 Festival of the Book when Rick Britton introduced me to his publisher, Mariner Media Publishing, in Buena Vista, and the unexpected connection to my past and some of the stories. "Mountain Mural," as depicted on the cover, once hung in Buena Vista at the Southern Seminary (now Southern Virginia University). My brother, Robert, was living there when he was killed in an auto accident. For years, when the sign to Buena Vista appeared on the highway, my thoughts went to my visits there and his death on the highway.

Now I have new memories to add and they are pleasant and supportive. Andy Wolfe committed himself to working with me and publishing my book. Rick Britton helped shape the manuscript and the rest seemed to fall into place with the skill and patience of Judy Rogers in editing and Emilie Davis designing the cover and layouts. They made me feel so at ease and I was excited at seeing their expertise at work. Others there welcomed me with a smile and offered help as it was needed. I feel like I have made new friends. Thank you.

Last but not least, I want to thank my three sons: Michael McNicholas of Dallas, Texas; Joseph McNicholas of Sacramento, California; and Bruce McNicholas of Seattle, Washington. As children, they gave me great joy. As men, (I must stop calling them boys), they continue to give me unconditional love and encouragement to keep on doing the unexpected.

Now I have two daughters-in-law, Amanda and Kora, and to my great joy and thanksgiving, I will be a first-time grandmother in October. My mind is racing with anticipation of story time and lullabies with a new special little one. Thank you, Joe and Amanda.

To you my new reader, thank you for selecting my book. I hope it meets your expectations and takes you to the place of your own precious memories.

■ Prologue ■

At the age of almost sixty, I began the journey that is continuing to this day, writing of my life in essays, poems, and vignettes; I learned along the way they are all memoirs. Slices of time as I remember—mostly of childhood places and happenings, some humorous, some wistful, some so painful—I have been amazed when the joy appeared again.

Sign at Pound, Virginia

■■■

Introduction

My Appalachian Mountains and my hometown, The Pound, in southwestern Virginia are written about with love, honesty and pride; although I had longings to see what was beyond the next ridge. I satisfied those longings with world travels. Now I time travel from the then to now and am richer emotionally and spiritually for the journeys.

This collection was written over a period of twenty years. Each piece was written to stand alone and was inspired by a different memory—sometimes joyful, funny and other times filled with sadness. About eight years ago, I was sorting and filing the pieces and spreading them out on the sun room floor. As I walked from piece to piece, I realized they were telling the story of my young life in a rather unorthodox way—by poems, vignettes, stories and essays.

I have poems of birth, death and a handyman who comes to pay a debt, by raking leaves, on a cold, rainy November morning. I have stories of family characters and love of family even as they long to make me over in "First Perm" and "Beauty Contest-50's Style."

I write of my father's feelings when he had to leave school at thirteen to work in the coal mines. "July Wash" reveals his regret and the devotion of a young girl to her father:

> *I scrubbed my father's back as we sat on weathered chairs under the grape arbor.*
> *Scrubbed away coal dust from pits and creases in his neck....*

Reading, music and movies have always been a natural part of my creative life and I refer to some favorites in, "Black is the Color" and "Sing Along." In a poem, "Falling in Love," I fall in love with John Wayne at twelve, Elvis at eighteen and now 007 and we are growing old together."

I think my independent spirit and curiosity comes through in "Lucky Girl" when I slip out of the house in the early morning to watch my dad and some deputies load a mentally ill colored woman into a car for a trip to the state mental hospital in Marion.

Portions of this collection deals with saying goodbye to members of my family as sudden death, accidents, and disease reduces our numbers at a steady rate and the wounds in my heart at their passing.

Some themes are universal in the way I have lived and dealt with them. I hope it connects with readers in some way as they go about the Patchwork of their own lives.

Trigg Baker, "Best Banjo Picker in the Area"
(Lena Cantrell's grandfather)

▪ Mélange* ▪

For generations
my father's people kept old ways,
hacked through mountains, totin' a load.
Abraham and Lucy built a cabin
on Bold Camp section of The Pound.
Cantrells spewed from their union.
                    Wild as cubs they were,
          raisin' crops, children, minding stills
                  was what they did best.
Stanleys lived across the mountain
Dulcena, sweet, was her name
She drew in this cub, James Milton;
Fitzhugh Lee, my dad, came forth.
              Maxwells – tall, firm and distant,
              became notorious as one Edith
                slew her father, Trigg.
                  Why did she do it?
                    No one told me.
Grandmother Venie counted losses,
a sharing brother who helped
with her orphaned children,
Baby Napoleon, dead at three.
              Her love was a *Baker* man
              with black hair and eyes,
          rode a "high stepping mare,"
            through swirling leaves
            with a banjo on his back.
      He died early with a song on his lips.
              Baker a name so common.
These dreamers wrote, sang
lived high drama;
maybe a cut above.

    Cantrell ▪ Stanley ▪ Maxwell ▪ Baker

       These names claim me.

**a French word meaning mixture*

◾ My Birth Day ◾

The bed was soaked with Mother's blood,
lightening tore the sky and water fell in giant gulps,
until fissures opened and new rivers raced
from the ridges gorging their drunken way down the mountainside
where they gushed and spewed into the Pound River that
rose, beat its banks, then with a roar
broke free and took over fields, small bridges, sheds and
a favorite basketball that bumped and bobbed its way to the Ohio,
while Mother listened for Dad and the doctor's steps
not knowing our footbridge was caught in this frenzy of tumbling,
yellow water, and
they were seeking an over-mountain pass to reach
the small weathered house, that rested at the neck of Maggard Holler,
and Mother who lay with a bloody, glistening newborn,
while her heart skipped beats and she longed to rest from
her labors and be tended.

Lena Cantrell in Maggard Hollow
c1938

◾ First Violets ◾

I walked in the garden today
and what do you think I saw?
Violets here and every where,
so beautiful and so blue.
You know what they reminded me of?
They reminded me of you.

When you were four or maybe more,
with pigtails—freckles and missing front tooth,
you brought me violets, again, and again
Clutched in a tight little fist.

Now you are a big girl,
and bring me violets no more.
I viewed them with a sign,
and a tear in my eye.
How wonderful God makes them grow!

Written by Mother, 1955
Tottie Baker Cantrell
1912–1997

◾ Too Many ◾

We sat at the supper table
while Dad spoke of the day.
Opened the *Bristol Herald*
and gave me the funnies.

I saw WAR DECLARED
bold and black!
War looked like an angry word
on half the page.

Would bombs come over here?
Who would keep them away?

Dad said, "Lots of our boys are gonna die
saw a line at the induction office and
I might have to go."

Dad had too many children
to be sent "over there."
Was five too many? Was it me?

Was it Mickey—too many?

■ A Lucky Girl ■

How could anyone in the whole world be so happy and not bust? I pumped my legs harder and this accented the clack clack as my skates made contact with the sidewalk, raced down Summer Street, and jumped a large crack as I neared home. My home was a special two-story, white-frame, maybe a Victorian house, with a stone wall in front and a deep porch. It was so close to the street, you could sit and talk normal to anyone who passed, without getting off your seat. Friends walking to and from town, liked to stand by the wall and comment on the war, weather, planting signs, or news of the boys away from home.

I really liked that I could sit under the apple tree at the side yard. Its branches shaded the far end of the porch, so I could sit quietly, listening to serious adult conversations while I read. I could do this trick: read, listen, and if a familiar name came up or they started to kinda whisper, I could tune right in and never move my eyes.

We had moved to Wise about three years ago when Grandpaw became the jailor of Wise County Jail. He needed Dad to help him, so the whole clan moved. Paw and Mammy Cantrell lived above the jail, and had lots and lots of rooms with many beds. Paw wore a wide leather belt, plaid shirts, and carried a big ring of keys everywhere he went. They opened doors and secret places in the jail.

Mammy Cantrell had a round sweet face, a shy smile, and eyes that hugged you. She had a welcome pat for everyone. "Honey, can you sit a spell? Can you have a bite to eat with us? Honey, fetch Sugarman a drink of cool water, and wrap up that piece of corn bread, put some butter and jelly on it now." Everyone loved Mammy and she loved them right back. She had lots of experience with loving and children. She had twelve, all of them living, and Daddy was the oldest.

I even had an Aunt a month younger than me. Martha didn't like for me tell this at school or around because lots of kids in town thought this was strange. I didn't. I thought it special and was a bit protective of this shy, doll-faced little Aunt, who had a difficult time adjusting to living in a town after her short lifetime spent in one of the "hollers" over the mountains in Bold Camp section near The Pound.

Everyone should be so happy to be alive and almost six, speeding along on fast skates, shining sun to warm your back on a cool, bright afternoon in April, almost Easter, and the best family in the whole wide world.

If only I could sneak in without Mother catching me for being so late. She liked to do that special switch trick on my legs. She switched and I would do the switch dance. "OW!" Hop-hop. Hop. "OW!" Hop. Sounded like the Easter Bunny, hop-hop-hop. "Ha! Ha!" Maybe this time she won't know how late it is.

With a jerky, bumpy stop, I turned, backed into the stone steps, and sat with a plop. I removed a skate key tied to a frayed, stained shoelace from around my sticky neck and proceeded to unlock my skates from the brown high-top shoes. I spit on my fingers a couple of times, and rubbed intently at the indentations left by the metal skate clamps. Taking a quick swipe at the scratched toes, I sighed, and blew up at my long bangs to cool my forehead. The hair settled in sticky clumps on my flushed face. Freckles stood on broad cheeks and round nose. I had tried mother's vanishing cream, and tobacco juice as well as buttermilk. Nothing seemed to work; the freckles just stayed and stayed. Shirley Temple didn't have freckles and everyone thought Shirley Temple was so cute.

Buckling the skate straps together, I stomped my tingling feet, skipped, and hopped up the stone steps to our home. Rising on tippy toes, I crossed the wide porch, grimacing as the screen latch snapped its little warning, stepped quickly into the warmth of the home, and paused to savor the warm thoughts of supper. "Ah, I love that smell!" Cornbread, cinnamon-laced cooked apples, and a pot of vegetable beef stew. "Maybe I can sneak a piece of bread and butter before suppertime."

"Lena, Lena Carol, is that you? Do you have any idea what time it is? It's almost five. You know you're supposed to be in at four-thirty. Where have you been all this time? Don't tell me—just out skating and visiting. You can waste more time just doing nothing than any child I know."

My mother, Tottie, appeared at the doorway of the bright spacious kitchen, and wiped her hands on a blue-checked apron. She looked intently at me standing quietly in the long hallway, gauging her temperament from a distance.

Shifting my feet slightly, I looked left then right then peeked through the long bangs, "No ma'am, . . . No ma'am I didn't. I didn't stop."

Mother continued to look at me with cool blue eyes, eyes that could see all, knew all, and reacted to all. I don't think mother ever slept, cause she knew everything about everyone in the household. If a sip of milk was taken from the glass bottle, she knew; if anyone dipped a finger in the jelly, she knew; if anyone touched the lotions and cream on her dresser, she knew. She knew everything!

"Well, I only went by to see if they still had that big colored woman there. No, I only skated up to the side door, and skated round and round on the porch. The office door was open, and Daddy was at the desk. I skated round and round and shouted, 'Is she still there? Is she still there?' Daddy nodded, and told me to get on home before I got in trouble, and to tell you not to wait on him for supper. That's exactly what I did. I did not stop for one second, I skated the whole time."

Like an incoming wave, I continued, "Do you think Daddy's safe? Do you think they got that woman locked up tight enough this time? You think she knows where we live? You think she ever killed anybody?"

"Lena, stop all this talking and worrying right now. She's locked up good and tight. Your daddy and uncle are strong men, and she is behind very strong bars, and thick, brick walls. The only reason she got loose was because your daddy has such a soft heart and doesn't like putting handcuffs on people. He can usually get them to come along quietly, 'cause he reasons with them and talks softly."

■ ■ ■

Sunlight filtered through soft lace curtains at two slender windows flanking a small fireplace with low burning coals. Light waned as it reached a white iron bed, hastily made, but eye-catching in color. Old Grandmother's flower garden quilt was folded neatly. I liked that name, "flower garden." You could have the bright colors of summertime even when it was cold and snow was flying. Just looking at it made you warm and safe. An open trunk held stacks of colorful clothing pieces, each stack a different shape and color. Reds, blues, greens, floral yellows, and small checks, even patterns so vivid you couldn't look at them very long or you would be drawn into a whirling mass of wind-like pieces of color.

A flat basket held some of the quilts in various stages of piecing. Each piece carefully joined another and another until a square was made and it could be attached to yet another finished square. It went on and on until a quilt top was complete. The fun was seeing these pieces of scraps—all left from dresses, blouses, shirts and jackets Mother made for us—and picking out your clothes, or asking, "Where did this piece come from, Mother?"

The trunk, basket, and pieces were always waiting when Mother found a few minutes to sit by the baby bed in this comforting room. She would sit, stitch, hold pieces to the light, and carefully select those for the next square. Her hands were strong and sure when she picked up the needle and thread. She took secret delight in their graceful shape and cared for them with a nightly ritual of Jergen's lotion.

Mickey's crib, a low oak rocking chair by the fireplace, an open Singer sewing machine with foot pedal, a small table with a bent, green lampshade with patterns of overlapping leaves, and Dad's large rolltop desk made this room so special.

I loved to lie on the large braided rug near the fireplace and under the crib. There I could gaze into the low flames, look up at Mickey and play all the games he liked. I could catch his hand when he would reach for me through the bars, tell him fanciful tales, and sing.

Mickey loved it all too, never cried to be taken out, just ran round and round the crib, called out his baby talk, and bounced from side to side as we played peek-a-boo. He twirled his tattered blanket 'round his head as he whirled to my singing, "Ring around the rosie, pockets full of posies, ashes, ashes, all fall down." With the last fall down, he would throw his hands in the air and fall with a squeal.

My heart would skip a beat and grow warm as I looked into the open, trusting face of this blonde, curly-headed angel among us. It was a fact that Mickey looked like a picture-book angel. When they strolled Mickey up the street, people would stop to pat his curls and say, "Law—look at him. Look at them curls. Look at them big blue eyes. Looks just like a little angel."

Mickey arrived in a deep soft snowstorm a couple of days after Christmas; carried in a large scuffed black bag that Dr. Sikes always had with him. I was not actually there when the bag was opened to see how folded he was, but saw him the next morning when I came home from Paw and Mammy Cantrell's.

Mickey's arrival in the black bag was a constant puzzlement, too, and I managed to get as close to the bag as possible when Dr. Sykes came to call on or check on some member of the family. I wanted to see if I could get a peek at the babies there or hear them cry. I couldn't understand how they could fit in such a small space with all the things Doc carried there. Maybe they were pressed flat or something. Mother would give me a firm look and say "Go along out and play. Don't linger near the door, or try to listen. Go on now."

When we finished the last "all fall down," we settled in for a peaceful time of thinking and looking at the coals in the fireplace, and occasionally touching Mickey's dangling hand from my resting place under the crib on the 'round-the-world braided rug. I thought it was 'round-the-world because if you started in the middle and walked your fingers, you could go round and round in large circles until you were out.

These quiet moments were occasionally interrupted by distant footsteps on the stairway, doors closing or David calling out from the hallway, "Hey Mother, what's for supper? I'm starving to death. Don't think I can wait. I gotta get over to the school and watch the football practice. Coach says I'm some kinda big boy and will be a good football player someday. Hey where's my jacket? Somebody's knocked it to the floor again—Lena's skates are hanging here. Why does she have to hang them up? Nobody hangs skates with the coats except her. She thinks more of those dadburned skates than I would if I had a horse, and I would think the world of a horse if I had one for sure. I wouldn't bring it up on the porch or nothin', just keep it in the barn, feed it, brush it, and ride it around the town and wave to everybody."

David was the third child and second son, and a study in motion—mental and physical motion. At nine he was often challenged at the nearby theater about paying a full price to enter. At twelve, full fare was required, and he was asked so much that he still paid child's fare long after the twelfth birthday. "That's David Cantrell, looks big for his age, must be almost six foot tall and weigh close to two hundred pounds. Gonna be some football player when he gets to high school, probably play in college or pro." People in town were always saying that kind of stuff about David. He just stuck his chest out more, and grinned like he owned the world.

David's eyes were hazel-green, but warm and smiling like Dad's, and his hair was brown with a hint of wave. He laughed loudly at himself and private jokes with his large gaggle of mismatched boys, all sizes who thought he was their best friend. He never went anywhere alone, and long before he would be ready for school or anything, they would drop by, hang around the stone wall, and call out: "Hey, David, you ready? Where we goin? What we gonna do? Let me throw some passes for you. When we chose up for Red Rover, pick me first."

Frances and Robert could be heard entering the house, hanging coats, tossing books, Frances going straight upstairs to the bedroom she and I shared, overlooking the street. Slender and pretty to beautiful, Frances, at thirteen, had little time to waste on the younger children; she had more important things to do before heading to the church for youth group. Her hair had to be brushed until it shone and arranged casually down each side of her face, so she could toss it to punctuate each sentence, when she got the chance to talk to four-houses-up, two-years-older, freshman in high school, football-playing, Creed Bruce. Swoon! All her friends swooned over Creed. His father owned the drugstore, so money had to be saved, scrounged to get the afternoon Coke there. Sometimes Creed took a turn behind the soda fountain, and held court before the preteens, mid-teens, and older teens. It was as if they had their own movie star here in Wise.

Wise is a small town, but a busy one, located in the extreme southwestern part of Virginia. Maybe a strange name for what was once a huge track of unexplored land. The first white man to cross into what is now Wise County and leave a written record was Captain Christopher Gist. Gist was a scout for George Washington. Gist crossed Pine Mountain after it was explored and named. So many people then to the present, know little or nothing of this section other than to think it is populated by a bunch of ignorant hillbillies. That name makes me so mad.

Robert, my oldest brother, entered more quietly than the others. Tall, slightly built with a hint of his later development into a six-foot-plus well-proportioned man. His thick, sandy hair grew low over a wide forehead. Dense eyebrows were a darker brown and perfectly arched. Clear skin, high cheekbones, and hazel eyes gave him a royal or princely look.

I heard the bedroom door swing wider and knew it was Robert checking on us. This was his first stop when he came home from school and ball practice. He saw Mickey sleeping, and gave me a slight wave and smile as I lazed by the fire. Straight, white teeth against finely defined lips. Robert looked contented. He ran his fingers through his hair with a sideways motion, lifting it, and smoothing it at the same time. He turned to go across the hall, check on supper and visit.

"Hi Mother, that smells good, really good—I love your beef stew. Yes, we had a long, hard practice. You know how coach wants us to be so good, so when the war is over, and the older boys come back we'll be ready to take on the whole county? When do you think it will be over, the war, Mother? Maybe a couple more months? Huh?"

"I don't mind playing so hard, even though I am in sixth grade; we might get to play cause we're so short on players. Everybody says I have a good chance. That would be really something to get in a game."

Robert put a stirring spoon in the stew, blew on it, and tasted it carefully. "Great, Mother, just great." He leaned his elbow on the corner of the warming unit of the black coal-burning cookstove, crossed his long legs, looking down at the well worn, polished shoes. Tied neatly, but creating painful jolts with every step. Knowing the family's situation on ration stamps for shoes, he hated to show his discomfort to his mother, thus adding to the ever-present worries of clothing and feeding this family of seven.

Sugar was one of the most difficult things for Mother to do without, for she loved to bake. When they had first arrived in Wise and before the rationings, she had won immediate respect at the local Methodist Church's socials with her butterscotch pies and angel food cakes. One taste and people would ask, "Who brought this? It's the best I ever tasted." She would just smile and say "Thank you." Mother didn't think it appropriate to show too much pleasure openly.

■ ■ ■

I opened my green eyes slowly, then quickly like a pop. Stretching my legs under the white chenille bedspread, I looked toward my sleeping sister. If Frances was looking my way, I planned to yawn and turn over. Usually she slept deeply, bunched under the covers, mass of brown curls under and over her pillow, head deep into the feather ticking mattress.

Sound asleep. She was always sound asleep in the mornings. Mother had to call her three times and send me back to tell her to get up. You never know, this just might have been the one time her sleeping clock went "Boing" and she changed right here into someone who wakes up early. That would just be my luck!

Still on my back and looking straight at the ceiling, I slipped my right leg from under the bedding and grabbed the edge of the railing with my right hand and began to scoot to the edge of the bed as quietly as possible. Inch by inch I scooted until I fell with a soft thump on the brightly flowered linoleum floor.

Shoot! Missed the rug again. It must have moved when Frances came to bed last night. If I ever do this again, I'll try to sneak a bigger rug from the boy's room across the hall. Cautiously standing, I gave another quick look at my sleeping sister and did a little victory hop. I reached under the bed for my lace-ups, and proceeded to put each one on with great concentration. Big loops and strong ties.

Robert had taught me well during the long, winter months, as we gathered in our parents' bedroom, before a blazing fire, listening to the latest war news on the big radio. The RCA usually stayed in the not-too-often-used parlor except during the winter, when they moved it to the bedroom.

I had to really concentrate and learned to lace, loop, and tie. I was determined and Robert was patient, because I knew if I could get my shoes off and on by myself, I could get dressed alone, be out and about, checking on things without waiting around for someone to find time for me.

Mother had a fit when I tucked the long strings into the sides of my shoes and clopped around until a string or two worked out. The results—muddy, wet, or frozen strings and scraped knees from the falls I would take if I forgot and tried to run up and down the steps.

OK, shoes done. I had dressed, at bedtime, in a long jumper, blouse, and sweater. Afterwards, putting my long flannel gown over all that, I finally settled in for a restless sleep. I had an internal clock that could wake me up anytime I wanted. That was especially handy at Christmas when I could listen for Santa Claus on the roof every thirty minutes or so and be the first one up.

Pulling my jacket from under the bed, I was ready. Dressed and ready. "Hope I can get there in time," I thought, as I quietly made my way across the slick floor to the door that opened to the hall. The floor gave a squeak, as I prepared to turn the brown marbled doorknob—slowly—slowly, with much concentration. My hand turned the knob and pulled slightly, hoping I could ease the click when it stopped. "I've just got to get there in time, just got to!"

Last evening, after supper, I overheard Daddy discussing the early morning trip he would make to take the colored woman to Marion. Something about being a place for "mental or metal people." Anyway, I wanted to be sure they got her into the car and that Daddy was safe.

Down the steps to the first floor, I had to get through the kitchen and out the back door without being discovered by Mother. Fortunately the door to the bedroom was closed, so I passed through the kitchen to the back-screened porch, then down the back steps, taking extreme care with each one. Walking quickly down the side path to the barn, I entered the alley that ran behind all the houses on Summer Street and came out on Main.

A couple of dogs barked, a rooster crowed, but no one was on the path delivering milk or checking on chickens. Turning left, I stood for a moment at the corner by Moody's Restaurant and peered down the street. Pink was showing in the sky, and complete daylight was near, so I ran. Ran past the drugstore, past the mercantile, past the shoe shop, and crossed at the courthouse. I thought my heart would jump out of my chest.

The jail and courthouse were separated by an expanse of green lawn. My destination was the center, where a cannon rested on a cement-and-stone base. I planned to stand behind the statue, where I could peek around and see the side entrance to the jail. This was where Daddy's office was, where prisoners were checked in, and close by the cells for women prisoners.

I didn't know where they'd put the screaming, colored woman last night. Maybe they put her in the middle room, a large cage in the center of the women's section. It had a bunk bed and was for those who were drunk and wanted to fight everybody.

Two deputy's cars were pulled up to the side porch, and I could see Uncle Luther talking and smoking with a couple of men I had never seen before. "We shore had a rough time gettin' her out the house. She's from over to East Norton, and she tore up a bunch of stuff at her Momma's. We've been over there before and usually Fitz can get her to settle down."

Her Momma scared her with police talk, and Fitz went along with it and told her to be good and she wouldn't have to get locked up. Seems like

somebody gave her some moonshine to drink. Thought it'd be funny seein'
what she'd do. She ain't never been right, but lately hear tell it's worse. We
always had a time gettin' her loaded without no cuffs. Fitzhugh's gonna get
it real bad one of these days."

I drew in a quick breath on hearing Daddy's name. Fitzhugh Lee Cantrell
was absolutely the best Daddy anybody ever had. He never got switches
after me; he let me visit the jail, told me about all the keys. Sometimes he
let me skate in the women's sections when they were empty. They were
empty a lot and that is why I was such a good skater, I could skate when it
rained and even when it snowed. But we did not—no did not—tell Mother
about that. No Sir.

The men at the door suddenly threw down their cigarettes and entered the
jail. I craned my neck, stepped out a little, and then quickly stepped back.

Suddenly, appearing at the doorway—or rather filling the doorway—was
this strange apparition. The mountainous colored woman, now clothed in
large bibbed overalls and red plaid shirt, was being walked and scooted
out with two men at each arm. Her head hung slightly to one side, and she
almost seemed to be sleeping. She began to moan loudly, "Where we goin'?
. . . Where we goin'? . . . Take me home! . . . Take me home! . . . Take me
home . . . NOW!"

They maneuvered her step by step to the nearest car, with its doors wide
open. Uncle Luther got in the back seat, sat very still, and watched as they
creeped and shuffled to the other door. I held my breath as they began to
sit her down in the seat. Luther pulled at her nearest arm and handcuffed
himself to her.

Daddy came down the jail steps, handcuffs in each hand, took a couple of
deep drags on a cigarette, tossed it, settled his hat firmly, then called out,
"Boys, you're doin' just fine. We'll have her loaded and over to Marion in no
time at all. Be back by suppertime."

Daddy walked round to Luther's side, leaned over his brother, saying
quietly, "Easy now, just easy now. Take this cuff quiet like and slip it on her
other arm and fasten it to the door. There. You got it? Good."

Luther looked doubtful at his older brother. "I don't know about this, Fitz,
I just don't know. You think we can hold her if she gets real wild again?

Why don't you just let that Doc from the state just knock her out? Then we'd have no worries. C'mon Fitz."

"Luther, the Doc gave her enough to keep her kind of quiet, but awake. I don't want any big harm to this poor soul. What a mess of a life. What a mess in the cell. She turned on the water last night and flooded the whole place. Paw just about had a stroke when he saw it, said, 'Boys, just load her up and get her out.'"

"I'm going 'round to the other side and let them cuff me. Just stay calm, and talk low."

The car was listing, and the back shook as Daddy began to take his place on the other side of this mound of black flesh. Someone removed his hat, tossed it in the front, and began to attach him to the other arm of the mumbling giant. "Oh Lordy . . . jus' take me home; jus' take me home."

From a distance, the car seemed filled with arms, shoulders, and heads. The arms would rise at different times as if waving or trying to fly. The red plaid shirtsleeves were attached on either side to pale white arms that appeared no larger than a child's. The flapping increased as the doors were closed and the motor started. Back tires appeared half flat, and the car seemed inches from the sidewalk.

"I think it's gonna sink," I thought, as the car backed toward my hiding place, before easing down the side of the jail to the back parking lot and on to Main Street leading out of town.

I saw Daddy's face frozen in strong determination, and Luther looking wildly toward his brother. "Lord help us."

People go to war and never come back, I thought. But can they just go down the road and never come back? Daddy would never do that, not if he could help it. I know he'll be back. What would we do if he didn't? I don't know what we'd do. We'd probably all lay down and die. Anyway, I got more to worry about now. How to get home without Mother finding out where I've been. I am sure to get the switching of my life if that happens.

Dear Jesus, don't let Mother find out.

Dad (Fitzhugh Lee Cantrell) at Wise County Jail

Tottie Baker Cantrell at Wise Court House
1942

Dulcena Stanley Cantrell and James Millard Cantrell
(Fitzhugh Lee Cantrell's parents)

▪ NO ▪

No—you can't hold the new baby

No—you can't get in the crib with him

No—you can't stay away from Sunday school and skate to the jail

No—you can't visit Dad (the jailer) and eat with the women prisoners

No—you can't leave the porch or yard, we are quarantined

No—Mickey won't die, he is sick with polio

No—you can't stay behind—we are all moving—to The Pound

No—you can't sleep on the porch with Fluffy
    or watch the puppies get born

No—you can't wade the river in front of the school

No—you can't bring that old box in the house or sleep in it

No—you can't sleep on my side of the bed—stay over there!!

No—you can't join the army

No—you can't sit on the bridge

No—you can't get a job, you're only eleven

No—you can't use the cash register—you can bag sugar and beans

No—you can't learn to drive—are you crazy?

No—you can't join the Boy Scouts—you can play ball
    if we're short of players

No—you can't stay up all night and read. Turn out that light!

No—you can't keep your pigtails;
    you're almost 13 and are wearing a bra

■ House by the School ■

The small frame house sat across the river from a massive '20s-era steel bridge on an unpaved road. It was white, one story, with a tin roof that sloped over the long, front porch. A swing to the right, a glider to the left, odd painted chairs randomly sat and easily moved.

The glider was a favorite courting spot of my only sister, Frances, and her sweetheart, James C. Roberson. He wanted to be a lawyer, and was a Republican. That was not an endearing title in our household, cause we loved Franklin Delano Roosevelt kinda like we did God. Well, James loved our dad and somehow he stopped wearing his Dewey button when he came around.

My youngest brother, Mickey, and I would often sit quietly in the living room by the low window behind the glider and listen. Now and then we would take a peek. If we caught a glimpse or shadow of an arm across the back of the glider, Mickey would inevitably get the giggles, Frances would yell for Mother, and we would scoot across the room trying to get to the back door before Mother appeared.

This porch was a good place to sit on a rainy day, a sultry day, or a sad day. Cars, trucks, and occasional horse and wagon, or people on foot would cross the bridge into The Pound.

Sometimes they waved and you could hear snatches of conversations, or the bridge would moan from heavy loads and clang with hooves and wagons. I loved this parade!

A low wire fence separated the front yard from the road, and a profusion of color framed the house or bridge. It depended on your viewing position. Dahlias and glads were tied to the fence with strings—then marigolds, nasturtiums, coxcomb. Then came roses, roses, roses.

On spring berry-picking trips, we would haul dirt from rotten logs or Dad would bring well-seasoned manure from the barn. I thought we had the richest, most colorful flowerbeds in the whole town.

At the back of the house was a smokehouse—later converted to a sleeping house with bunk beds and a fireplace—and a low, long grape arbor. A terrific place for staging shows—especially my "Carmen Miranda" number with real grapes, plastic bananas snitched from the back porch table, and pressed funeral-wreath ribbons for a colorful skirt and halter.

"Aye, ya, ya, I like you verry much. Aye, ya, ya, I think you grand." Now that was a song and a dance!

My oldest brother, Robert, would make the announcements. He could swallow four grapes, then bring them back up. He also told scary stories about monsters under the bridge. He would coat his mouth with the newest in dental care—chlorophyll toothpaste—and proceed to have a falling down "fit." Mother would get calls about that one. Sometimes we could toss Mickey and the smaller kids on a blanket until they screamed and got all red in the face, until someone told us to "stop that right this minute."

A low coal shed was slanted at the end of the arbor. Just a plain, wood coal shed. It was often my second brother's chore to get coal for the kitchen stove and the warm morning heater. David was my "Hoss Cartwright" of a brother—looks, personality, and big heart.

In the winter months, he usually waited until after dark to get the coal in, and had a great fear of night as well as the coal shed. He would persuade me to go with him to carry a light and admonish me to hold the light very steady. The shadows cast on the darkened walls of the shed made him work fast and cast his eyes around fearfully.

Upon leaving the shed, I couldn't help if occasionally my hand would shake, and trees, arbor, and smokehouse would take on grotesque shapes. Sometimes coal would fall from the buckets, as Dave would scoot like a crab to get into the house safely. As we grew older, he was less inclined to have me accompany him with the light, so he would sing loudly, mournful country songs. "Never cared much for singing the blues, da-dada-da-da-dada, that I'd ever lose your love." People could hear him from the edge of town.

Our garden stretched from the arbor to the back of the lot where we had a barn and pigpens. A narrow path followed the garden on the left. When corn was high it hung over the path and scratched my arms and legs every time I passed. Running made it worse—it would sting. I often had red welts on my arms, legs, and face from the many trips made to gather eggs, slop the pigs, feed the chickens, and check to see if the barn cats had any new kittens.

Many evenings I would go with Dad or Robert when they went to milk the cow. There I would sit in the loft at the end of the stall, swing my legs and talk, talk, talk. Sometimes they laughed. They thought I was OK; good company, and they never told me to wash my face, straighten my collar, or do something with my hair! They let me take a learning turn at the teats, and Dad would give me a ride on his back down the path home. Mother would always say, "Fitzhugh put her down—you know she's getting too big to carry!" Dad would smile quietly and reply, "Ah, Tottie, I just don't like to tell her no."

Grandmother Venie with grandchildren:
Back row: Lena, cousin Walt Ellison, David
Front row: Frances holding cousin "Twiggie" Ellison,
Mickey, Grandmother Venie holding cousin Sandra Robinson,
cousin Kenneth Ellison, Robert holding cousin Aaron Ellison,
and our dog, Fluffy
c1947

David Cantrell
1946

▦ ▦ ▦

Michael (Mickey) Cantrell
1951-52

▦ ▦ ▦

Frances and Lena Cantrell
in Pound, Virginia

▦ ▦ ▦

James C. Roberson
(future brother-in-law, lawyer and judge)

▦ ▦ ▦

◾ Oasis ◾
Childhood

In my childhood,
I sat by windows
on cold December days,
Looked out on barren trees
nude mountains,
etched against gray
uninviting sky,
as bitter angry winds
whistled through the valley
across the river
entered the room
by unseen pores
and fissures
chilling my back.

I sat with
thick stockened legs
slung over
fat arms of
overstuffed chair
toasting my feet
on coal burning stove.

My mind's window saw
and dreamed of
white sanded beaches
perpetual sun,
trees that moved to
dancing winds.

Rocking oceans
carried me
to lands where people
moved quickly
spoke musically
smiled widely
then waved at me
to join them!

■ A Letter to My Brother's Children ■

Dear Charlotte, Fitz, and Robbie,

The following narrative is not intended to cause you pain or sadness in remembering your father, my brother Robert Cantrell, it is just my wish to share some of my vivid memories of our young lives as we grew up in our mountain town, deep in the heart of Appalachia. These memories, emotions and dreams are with me constantly since my return to care for Mother. She could not accept the reality of his death and retreats more and more into the balm of forgetting everything.

I am trying to heal and find ease from my own pain at the death of your father, death of my husband, and in the past year the sudden death of brother David. My strong, vital, bigger-than-life "Hoss" of a brother, David. With my sons grown and away in distant colleges in Texas, California, and Maine, I gave up a way of life and identity I had known for almost thirty years, living in far-away countries, to now return to my beginnings and tackle this restoration of Litchfield Hall. Have I lost my mind? Limited resources and little knowledge of historic homes make this sound like another of "Lena's wild dreams."

I am constantly amazed at the way old memories have taken over my dreams and thoughts. They entertain me for hours as I scrape, paint, haul debris, hang wallpaper, dig, plant, and engage in the endless chores involved in restoring this 125-year-old house here in Abingdon, Virginia. Dreaming, working, and planning the next project are apparently the right prescriptions, for I look forward to the sunrise and what the day will bring along with scarred hands, tired legs, and aching back.

These fragments and scenes from our family life—places, events, and characters we knew—are so vivid, I can smell the oil of the school's wooden floors, see the dimly lit interior of Henry I's old general store, watch bees lazily circle Mother's lush flowerbeds, feel the chill wind through my hair as I ride here and there on my bike, see the Sunday dinner spread before us, recall specific conversations, and feel so enveloped by all of it, that upon waking or returning to awareness, I want to retain it, hold it, savor, and remember each cherished detail. Sometimes slowly, other times quickly, it all fades—no matter how hard I try to hold the essence with all my being.

So, this morning, I awoke with this letter to you children at the center of my consciousness. I lay in bed in the early a.m. startled at the clarity of what had unfolded during my deepest sleep. I jumped up, ran down to the study, searched frantically for anything to write on, and found a red-bound ledger (with "1987" on the cover). I rarely throw anything away, thank goodness! Settling myself in the old Boston rocker by the kitchen stove, new advertising pen in hand—"Step Back in Time With a Stay at LITCHFIELD HALL," circa 1869—I began. Indulge me while I tell about your father and how important he was to me in my childhood.

Robert was the oldest boy and I the fourth child and second girl. There was a difference of five years in our ages. Our birth order was Frances, Robert, David, me, and Mickey.

I recall living in nearby Wise for a few years before returning to the town where we and our ancestors had lived for generations. During those early years, Robert taught me to ride a bicycle; he put me on the seat, gave me a shove and said, "Stay on." Not knowing about brakes and such, I would jump off when it was time to stop. He taught me how to put on and tighten my skates, and jump bumps in the sidewalks. I was a racer! I mastered high-top shoes, the tying, and loopy bows. He never ran out of patience.

This morning's dream was of the day we returned to The Pound and the house by the school, Christopher Gist High School, at the edge of town. The house sat across the river from a massive '20s-era steel bridge, on an unpaved road. The bridge was the entrance into the town, and some people seeing the family unloading, came over to speak and welcome Mother and Dad back home.

As I watched our possessions being unloaded and settled in new places, I became anxious and wondered where I would sleep, where my clothes and books were. I was especially fearful about finding a friend. Would I find one here? Would anyone like me here? I would enter second grade, and had heard they had strict teachers. I was seven and Robert was twelve on that moving day, and he surely had concerns and fears of his own, but he took the time to tell me not to worry, help locate my doll, and reassure me that I would find friends. He would be my friend 'til I found a new one.

Feeling reassured, I took Dolly and went for a walk on the schoolyard. I took a walk down the paved sidewalks at the lower edge of the long lot that ran parallel to the dirt road and river.

It had rained that day and the rain had mixed with drifting dirt from the road and formed soft layers of silty mud at the lower side of the walk. I had a great time singing and walking slowly, making squishy footprints, then counting them as I walked the length of the walk back and forth—back and forth. Another great thing about that walk, was the way it was covered with the foliage of a dozen or more tall, silver maple trees. They created a wonder world with filtered light and flashes of silver as the wind turned the leaves. The light varied with the seasons and the color of the leaves—I never grew tired of playing there. (Eventually, I made a tree house of cardboard boxes where I spent many summer days and evenings hidden away.) Raindrops continued to fall as each little breeze stirred the leaves, and I got wet as I studied the long stone school building from a distance.

Mother sent Robert to find me, but when he took one look at my mud-spattered clothing and body, he knew I was in trouble—big, big trouble. Somehow the mud got softer the longer I stayed and my feet just had to run or jump now and then.

Robert took me to the upper edge of the garden by the barn, went for a bucket of water, and did his best to get the mud from my face, arms, and legs. The evening wind was drying it as fast as he could wet it down, so he found some dried cornhusks we could use as scrapers.

When we arrived at the house, we entered through the back porch, but Mother saw us immediately. She was looking so frazzled and lost, that I felt badly adding to her frustrations, but she pounced and told me in no uncertain terms how she felt, how hard she had worked to get us settled, and here I was such a mess! Such a mess! Where would she find clean clothes?

Oh! How I hated that look, and that voice, and what usually followed. A keen switch on bare legs is no laughing matter, and there were lots and lots of trees in our yard and at the school. I knew I was gonna get a good one, and no time to pray.

Robert looked at my frantic face and Mother's stance and said the most unbelievable thing, "Mother, why don't you just give me the whipping, just give it to me." I thought I was hearing things. Was he crazy? Didn't he know how that hurt and made red knobby welts on your legs?

The plea was not completely successful, but it softened her momentarily, for I got a few quick swats with her hand and was sent to find some clean clothes and take our younger brother Mickey for a walk.

I was gone in a flash, found the red wagon, and took Mickey for a tour of the new playgrounds. Round and round the upper walks we went, carefully avoiding the lower muddy sections. I knew I was a splash away from a good switching.

We checked the entrance to the schoolyard, a maze of large round bars that you could enter, climb on, slide under, hang by your knees on, or just sit and pretend.

Mickey and I played until we were called in for a quick supper of thick bologna sandwiches and Pepsi, a treat usually saved for washdays.

Someone had put the porch swing up, and we sat, ate our sandwiches, and night fell around us. I then saw the bridge for the first time in the twilight, and heard the chorus of frogs that lived under it. A tinge of fear along with the cool mountain air caused a shiver to run through my body.

When I spoke of this fearful feeling, Robert began to tell us a fanciful story of giant frogs that lived under the bridge. Gauging our reactions, he continued, "Now, you better be careful and not cross at dark, cause they will jump out and eat you up."

Oh my! Where had we moved? What was this awful place with frogs that would eat you? I wondered if Mother and Dad knew about them. Surely they wouldn't have brought us here to this place, if they had known. Robert assured me they knew, but wanted him to explain about the dangers of crossing the bridge at night.

A full moon came up, mountain darkness descended, and the frogs continued in their tormenting chorus. Mickey had fallen asleep before the end of the storytelling, so for the moment he was spared the horror and dread of those monster frogs. When it was bedtime I asked Robert to please check my room to see if any frogs had entered and were waiting for me. His response, on seeing I was truly worried, was that if they came into the house, they would bring candy and ice cream because they didn't like to eat children in houses. Could I trust him?

Slightly relieved, I entered the house, got ready for bed, all the while listening to the frogs, and praying they stayed where they were and would not creep up the riverbank and cross the road—I didn't like to think of more!

So that was the beginning of scary stories, child-eating frogs, monsters, "hants" and anything that would give us a fright. Mickey and I became immune to his tales of horror, but we were delighted when a new audience of neighborhood children found their way to our yard or porch, on most evenings, for a good scare.

A few parents objected to their children being subjected to those evenings of fright; as most would not cross the bridge after dark to go home alone.

So you see, Charlotte, Fitz and Robbie, why the summer of 1943 is planted in my memory forever, and your father's influence in my life is constant.

Your loving Aunt,
Lena

▪ My Favorite Place ▪

Lena Cantrell
Miss Hughes
3rd Grade
English

My Favorite Place

Everybody knows that my favorite place is where I am right now. I am in my tree house. It is not a real house, but it is a real tree—a maple tree. Daddy says it is a silver maple tree. That is a good name because at night it looks silver when the moon shines on it. It looks silver when the wind blows. I like being in the moving, silver leaves.

There are thirteen silver maples here at the school. They are beside the long walk. They keep the walk cool. People like to sit under them at recess. My favorite is Number Four. I can hook my leg over a low branch and reach for a high limb to climb to the middle where I have my house.

My house is really a box. It is a refrigerator box—a Maytag box that has a big arrow. The arrow points "this way up." I cut a hole for my door, and some leaves stick into the roof. Sometimes rain and dew drips on my books and things.

I like to look at everything from this high place. I like to see my family's house by the school fence. I can see Mother when she hangs clothes on the line. The wind blows them, and blows her hair. It blows her dress. I laugh. She can't see me.

I like to move to the higher branches and look at the bridge that crosses the river into town. The bridge is tall and strong. It is made of steel. Even German bombs couldn't knock it down. I like to see the cars and trucks cross it. I can hear the clangs. Sometimes I see people I know walking. I wave and shout, "Hello, hello!" They can't see me. I laugh.

I don't like to look at the bridge when it begins to get dark. My brother says giant frogs live under it. He says they eat children if they cross at night. I never cross the bridge then. No! No! Never. I have never seen the giant frogs, but I hear them every night. They sound mad. Maybe they are hungry. I don't care. They can stay hungry. They can't get me up there. Ha! Ha! Ha!

On a hill beyond the bridge is a cornfield. I like to see the yellow corn tassels and shiny stalks. Sometimes they look like soldiers. Other times they look like dancers. I hum then. They always look like something else, just like clouds never look like clouds all the time.

I can see most of the church, high up on the hill that is in the middle of town. The church is wood with a tall steeple and two doors. The white church looks so good when the sky is blue. I like to look at it for a long time. Sometimes I am in the tree on Sunday when they ring the evening bells. I feel happy when the bells start, and sad when they stop.

Sister says I cry too much at silly things. That's the way I am. My tree and my house don't care. They fold me in, and I feel safe.

■ Grandmother Venie ■

I have wanted to write about my Grandmother Venie Maxwell Baker for a long time but was afraid I could not capture her essence or bring her to life again. Whatever is written needs to be carefully thought out because she could not abide falseness in anything.

Her children did not consider Mammy Baker an affectionate person. Her daughters would say, "Hold still Momma, I want to give you a hug." She would shove slightly with her folded arms and declare, "Ah, shaw—who's got time for such foolishness, all this huggin' and kissin'?" This was such a contrast to her instant liking of "Days of Our Lives," when TV came to the mountains and she acquired a set. "That is the mushiest bunch I ever saw. All that huggin' and kissin'. But that Rachael will get her comeuppance one of these days." As Mammie gave her familiar spiel about "mushiness," a hint of smile would try to stay in place as she tightened her lips. A mischievous glint would appear in eyes as blue as Scottish heather.

I loved Mammy for her strength, her lack of self-pity, and her easy ways with me. Never suggesting I needed to change anything or clean up. Her philosophy was simple: "Ain't no need to spend days frettin' over things that are done and gone and a body can't do a thing about. Keeps you from getting' a good night's sleep."

I was the fourth child of her oldest daughter, and was always ready for her company and sleepover nights at the old home place along the river with sharp mountains rising behind. We would walk from our home in town into the chilled summer air and take a little-used path around the side of the mountain to the mouth of Bold Camp section of The Pound.

Mammy called this little road "The Nars." Many years later I learned it came from a Scottish phrase, "the narrows," meaning a narrow path.

If we walked after dark in late fall, she would carry a carbide miner's lamp to light our way, but she was so sure-footed she could have walked it in the darkest of nights without a mishap or stumble. As we walked side-by-side, I would hold her dress and peer over the steep bank to the river below and pray we would not tumble. I liked the smoky light because we often heard the baying of hounds or night creatures and the wind would catch these sounds and send them flying and resounding. I could picture giant creatures or "hants"—mountain spirits or ghosts—waiting around the next bend or rushing down the cavernous hollers. The light was somewhat reassuring but the eerie circle it made only fueled my imagination as to what might be ahead. I loved to be scared—a little.

I never saw Mammy sad or tearful, and as I got older and learned more of her and our family history, I realized she did not speak much of the past, her childhood, marriage, or milestones of the passing years. She seemed to always live in the moment.

I learned she suffered greatly at the death of her young husband, and toddler son, of pneumonia. The murder of one brother brought the outside world into her life with microscopic reporting and sensational misrepresenting of mountain life and its people. When Edith Maxwell was tried for the murder of her father, Trig, sorrow and the lack of his support and presence changed the life of Mammie and the family forever. A widow with six children to raise and educate. She said, "I never would bring a strange man into my house who might have been bad to the children. I've seen some awful things happen with that, besides I'm still waiting for my cowboy."

If she commented on a handsome man she might say, "There's a fine specimen. I always like a man with dark wavy hair and pearly white teeth."

Mammy and I were fans of Saturday afternoon westerns that came to the local theater. She was partial to Gene Autry and thought he was real manly. "Gene is my idea of a real cowboy. That Roy seems a bit of a sissy in all that fancy white get-up. I don't think a real cowboy would be caught dead in that."

I liked Roy Rogers best and thought he was so handsome all in white, and Trigger was like something out of a fairy tale as they rode across the plains with his mane and tail flowing like ocean spray. They moved like one body as they came to sliding stops or Roy leaped to catch a hanging branch to wait the passing of bad guys. He would pull down three or four with a flying leap. Trigger always knew to seek out a nearby grove or scrub brush to await Roy's whistle.

We smiled and chuckled as we discussed our favorites and the latest feats we had witnessed them perform in the flickering light in black and white. We loved their songs and singing and I must admit I liked when either of them gathered around the campfires and sang of dusty trails, happy trails, and sunsets in the western sky. Such a pretty picture was enough to bring tears to my eyes at times.

"I'm going out west someday and find me a real cowboy and bring him home—how about that? Just watch and see if I don't."

Another of her favorite sayings was a reply to any inquiry to how old she was, "I'm thirty-nine and old enough to know better."

Bedtime on a normal Friday or Saturday night was 'round five or five thirty. I didn't mind this so much in the wintertime, but in the summer I would coax her to the porch with a head rub or promise of brushing her hair or a new hairdo. Her thin strawberry blonde hair was streaked with white, and not very long. Just enough for her to twist or gather into a knot at the back of her head with a couple of hairpins. Just the same, I would plait braids and wind them round her head, or wet her hair and make pin curls to see if it would be wavy when I took it down. I wanted her to look like some of the movie stars who had hair that waved over one eye. For some reason, I could never get that effect.

I felt so peaceful and happy when we sat on her porch high on the side of the hill in early summer evenings and rocked side by side. We could hear the cowbells in the distance as the cows shuffled around, settling under the trees for the night. Sometimes we sang old hymns and funny songs. "Precious Memories" and "When the Roll is Called Up Yonder" were a couple that fit the evening and the setting of the sun just fine.

One of our favorites was nonsensical and made you feel like clapping and dancing. It was about a man called "Old Dan Tucker."

> *Old Dan Tucker was a fine old man*
> *Washed his face in a frying pan,*
> *Combed his hair with a wagon wheel,*
> *Died with a toothache in his heel.*

While we sang this part Old Joe, her white lab, would doze but as we rocked faster in anticipation of the chorus, he would begin to thump his tail and open his eyes.

Get out the way Old Dan Tucker
You're too late to get your supper.

We sang loudly and rocked faster, and sometimes I would make my rocker scoot across the weathered floor to the railing and Old Joe would thump his tail and lift his head and howl.

When the evening chill appeared at the early setting of the sun, we made ready for bed. Mammy put her teeth in a glass of water beside the bed, and her mouth sunk in like a small hole, and her words came out like a stranger from another world.

She fell asleep immediately and would begin to blow softly from her puckered mouth with each breath. "Pssst-ta." I would slip my book from under the bed, lean on the windowsill, try to read by the fading light, and hope the moon would stay bright until I finished a chapter of my Nancy Drew mystery or the newest issue of *The Bobsey Twins.*

Her teeth and the moon were good company in the summer darkness and I felt like the safest girl in the world.

No character sketch of her would be complete without additional comments: Her straight neck and back, and the way she carried herself like royalty on display, or her love of a good milk cow and a warm glass of milk freshly strained and frothy. Her one cup of coffee a day was a half-cup of grounds boiled in a green spatter ware pot for several minutes and allowed to set until the grounds settled. When it was properly enhanced with several spoons of sugar she would comment, "I don't understand people needing to drink coffee all day long. One cup a day does me just fine." Oats and home-canned blackberry jelly with creamy hand-churned butter and hot biscuits were her breakfast for as long as I knew her. She loved walking and walked the trip to town once or twice a day to check on who was out shopping, and catch up on gossip at the post office. When offered a ride she might comment, "Thank you very much—but why don't you step out of that fancy car and walk a little beside me. Looks like you could do with a little exercise. A body can get mighty stiff if they don't stretch their legs a bit."

Everyone was startled at how Venie took to the soaps and especially "Days of Our Lives." Rachael and the others of the cast became her close friends and she would leave anywhere when time for the show appeared. She would rush home and rock away while she watched their lives unfold, and comment the next day to what mischief they had been up to or how she wouldn't allow that under her roof.

When a person you love is gone there is nothing that can truly bring them back, but in writing this piece, I have lived a little with Mammy Baker by my side again.

Grandmother Venie Baker in the yard
at Pound, Virginia

▪ July Wash ▪

I scrubbed my father's back
as we sat on weathered chairs
under the grape arbor.
Scrubbed away coal
dust from pits and creases
in his neck.

Lifebuoy—strong, pungent
foamed frothy as
I swished water
round and round
the old enamel pan
chipped here and there.

Dad would say,
"You can't scrub
too hard now
stuff sticks like glue,
you can't never get
shed of it."

I used a worn washrag
sized just right for
young hands to wring—
swish, wash and wring;
happy, pink bubbles
rose, floated, popped
in warm July dusk
as water stilled
into a gray, silent, pool.

Once Dad told me
when he was a child
mining coal
he cried into his lunch pail
salty tears, that
trickled and washed
his face
as he thought of his
empty desk,
and Silence answering
the teacher when she
called his name,
Fitzhugh?

Most times Dad
would light
a Camel,
take a hungry draw,
cough deeply
as he looked proudly
on the ripening garden.
Gazing upward to
the mountains beyond,
"I feel better already."

▪ Family Portraits ▪

Great Aunt Lockie
had a "problem."
I knew this at an
early age by
whispers about contents
of a large, black bag
carried over her crooked arm with
black scarred veins.

Whispers—"Lockie—you know
takes pills—takes stuff—
takes dope—a dope fiend."
That's what I heard.

She worked in Kentucky—
Jenkins post office
rode the Greyhound
over the mountain,
weekend visits in Pound
fried chicken dinners
with relatives.
She owned railroad stock
wore black underwear.

Paw sat
in the adjunct kitchen on
sagging cushions, ancient recliner
"earnin' his keep," so he said,
peeling potatoes
to drop into a lard can
of cold water—
French fries for
The Jerky Café!

Uncle Thurman
could not read
or write his name.
Years ago he would
drink, "lay out"
in the woods
'til morning sun
rose over foggy, fall mountains,
lit his face lying sideways
in damp leaves.

He sidled into the kitchen
where Mammy Baker
poured strong, black coffee
into a thick cracked cup
thumped it down
"Humph!"

■ Black is the Color of My True Love's Hair ■

Pie Supper 1948

Jamie Roy Mullins entered my life when outlying communities sent their students to Pound Elementary at the beginning of our sixth grade year. Until that time, they were in smaller (sometimes one-room) schools in Flat Gap, Mill Creek, Indian Creek, Mullins Creek, Dotson, and a variety of other places, for obvious and not so obvious reasons. This was quite a transition for everyone, as these schools were in the heart of isolated mountain settlements in the harsh Appalachian Mountains of Southwest Virginia, a short distance from the Kentucky state line. Each had distinctive characteristics, leading families, and history. What a difference five or ten crooked miles could make!

My actual awareness of him was not too clear until one day he told Tommy Morris to stop pestering me and leave my pigtails alone. Tommy sat behind me in one of the old style, (attached) wooden desks, where each desk joined the one in front until a row was formed. Tommy's fascination with my foot-long braids consisted of tying them in knots, untying the ribbons, sticking pencils and rolled paper through the plaits, and sometimes just pulling on them. Ouch!

Jamie was in the row across from Tom and could observe this constant jiggling of seat, pulling of hair, and general twelve-year-old male behavior toward the opposite sex. No one had ever told Tommy to stop anything because his father was principal of the school. On one level he knew this, and on another he frantically wanted to be treated like everyone else. Impossible, but we tried.

Tommy and I were friendly adversaries from the day my family returned to Pound from a four-year absence while we lived in the nearby town of Wise. I returned to begin second grade and met him that summer. We went to Sunday school together, taking the shortcut up the steep bank to the white, wooden-steepled church that prayed over the whole town. We ran free, played tag, climbed on the metal bars on the school grounds that were adjacent to my home. Our mothers were leaders and teachers in the church; our fathers became friends, played endless games of intense Rook, and replayed Friday night basketball games quarter by quarter. Our siblings were in classes together. It was a given, Tommy Morris teased Lena Cantrell. Four Eyes, Specks, Leapin' Lena, and Lena the Hyena—these were just a few of the choice ones. So I was very impressed when someone had the nerve to tell Tommy to back off.

I took a good long look, and this is what I saw. A tall, lanky, easy-moving young boy. He had thick, black wavy hair, brown eyes, wide shoulders and an assurance that is found in natural athletes even at such an early age. Baseball, basketball and football all appeared easy as Jamie later moved from the dirt playground to diamonds, courts, and fields. He became a star in all of them and scouts came later to check out this mountain player.

I think it was that moment, when he casually told Tommy to take it easy, that I fell in love with Jamie. Fell in love with the easy smile and unwavering way he looked into my eyes. This love would span years, influence future loves, die a natural death, and forever remain in my heart as my first love. It was never consummated but developed into a warm and supportive friendship that lasted through the uneasy days of adolescence, pranks, and escapades that reflected our common streak of minor rebelliousness.

We stood proudly together at graduation for a final picture as our parting began. At times I would ponder on "what if?" but knew in the deepest recesses of my heart that it was not our destiny to have more. I wondered would it have lasted so long, or been so influential in my life if it had grown into a mutual love.

The valentine was my first inkling that he might like me—it was the fold-over type with an envelope, not the punch-out ones that were sixty for a dollar. The message was clear—"I Want You to Be My Valentine." I was startled when I read it as we sat at our desks during the valentine party and the designated postman delivered it from the gaily decorated valentine box.

We had worked after school the week before, covering the box with red crepe paper, and cutout lace doily designs. It brightened the whole room and quickened our hearts at the messages it would hold.

Our teacher, Miss Emma Qualls, loved her students, loved teaching, and loved to let us arrange seasonal parties. Her enthusiasm for fun was contagious—classes seemed to fly by and learning was exciting. We learned to spell with Friday spelling bees, and had jubilant games of baseball—

pitching states and capitals while she ruled and beamed with apple cheeks and bubbling laugh.

After glancing at Jamie's card, I was fearful that Tommy would read it over my shoulder, make some teasing comment and everyone would notice. More horror, could Jamie see me read it, and could he see that my face was suddenly as red as the paper on the box? I would not look at him. I willed myself to keep my eyes focused on the front of the room or out the window to the snow-covered hillside.

The room buzzed with happy recipients of tentative messages of valentine love, and the counting began. Who got the most? Who signed them, "With Love"? Who got one unsigned? Who had a crush on who? I wanted to keep this a secret, but could I?

In the following days, I would not look at him openly, but managed sideways glances, over-the-top-of-the-textbook peeks, and avoided his row when I would lead the class in singing "Skip to My Lou," "Home on the Range," or "Down in the Valley." Sometimes I was not quick enough and he would smile in that slow, easy way that would cause my heart to contract with a new warm feeling, and my hands to grow moist. When we would play ball on the dirt courts at recess—boys at one hoop and girls at the other—I was aware of his every movement at any given moment, and I began to suspect he was equally aware of mine.

How did the others find out? Suddenly my best friends Irene and Shirley were teasing, and asking if I had a crush on Jamie. At first I denied any such thing, but they were not so easily fooled as they were more experienced in crushes and could read me like the neon sign I had become.

That spring the Boy Scouts had their annual pie supper at the old elementary school near the Methodist Church on the hill overlooking the town. I think that was the first year I took a pie, or rather the first year I was allowed to take one. Maybe sixth grade was a turning point in such things. We had unwritten codes and customs in these mountains, and "pie suppers" were probably an Appalachian version of a "coming out party." Mother made her notorious butterscotch pie (my favorite) and everyone knew what a wonder baker-cook she was; her mouth-watering productions were eagerly awaited at social events. To be complimented as having a "best dish" of anything caused many women to walk taller and smile secretly for days afterwards. I wore a new blue sweater (not a hand-me-down), that filled out with twin mounds of approaching maturity, navy blue skirt that swirled a little when

I walked, and fuzzy blue socks to match the sweater. A visiting Aunt had done my hair in French braids—more grownup than long pigtails that hung down my back. I felt lighter, brighter, and could not contain a broad smile as I dressed for the evening's event. "Black is the color of my true love's hair." The words of that old ballad would go through my mind each time I looked at Jamie, and now I felt like I might just sing it aloud for the world to hear.

My outfit had been purchased with earnings from my first job. I was bag girl and general gofer at the local grocery store, the Mick or Mack. This made it special, and it didn't have a ruffle or lace anywhere. I didn't look so healthy or young with this new look, but the freckles still sprinkled across my nose and face, and the little space between my two front teeth bothered me at times when I smiled. I had not adopted Mother's habit of placing her hand in front of her mouth. She pinched her lips together a lot because her space was much wider than mine, but she was afraid that mine would grow wider with age. I had so many new worries now; I would have to think about that later.

Jamie was there in his starched Scout shirt; red kerchief set off the clarity of his perfect skin and black hair. He was beautiful! He was handsome! All this had not gone unnoticed and girls in the seventh and eighth grades could be seen calling out to him on the playground, talking and giggling with him in line for the buses. These girls wore waist cinchers, Tangee lipstick, and Max Factor pancake makeup. Most noticeably, an older redhead was standing beside him when I entered with my pie. Her tussled curls bounced and jiggled as she swayed and shifted, then she rolled her black-fringed blue eyes like a movie star each time she looked up at Jamie. My French braided hair seemed to tighten like knots on my scalp with each step I took across the freshly oiled floor.

Everyone gossiped, jostled, and eyed prospects from across the cleared room. Pies were dramatically displayed on a large table at one end of the room, and printed cards identified the owners. My heart began to pound with an erratic beat, my throat and lips felt dry, and my mind began to jump. What if no one buys my pie? What if one of those old men buys it, will I have to eat with them? "I wish I had stayed home," kept coming in like a refrain. Who would pay money to eat pie with me? Sometimes older men bought pies for high prices to take home, especially if they were baked by a good cook. Please, please, don't let this happen!

I looked around. There were five cousins, one brother, one uncle and five boys who were such close playmates, like Tommy; I knew they wouldn't shell out a penny for my pie. This was for crushes and girls they wanted to impress. There were a couple of tough-looking boys from Mill Creek—one had used an obscene word at the Saturday matinee. He had leaned over my seat and whispered right in my ear, "Will you ___ me?" He was too repulsive for words, and if I had hinted to my brother, David, what he had said, that kid would have been mincemeat pie in seconds. What if he bid?

We did the cakewalks with couples paying a dime to walk around the table while the corner record player scratched out "Buffalo Gals," "Oh Susanna," or "Beautiful Dreamer." The couple standing the nearest to the selected cakes when the music ceased were the winners. At times it got a little rowdy as couples sped up and slowed down—they tried to anticipate when to stop.

Scout Leaders gave the awards. Then the bidding began. Chocolate, lemon, apple, and chess pies were lifted high and bids were called out. "SOLD! SOLD! SOLD!" rang 'round and 'round as the room darkened and lights were turned up.

My heart would not slow down as I saw Mother's butterscotch lifted. The piled meringue glistened in the fading light like caramel-tipped clouds. The bids went fast from $.15 to $.25 to $.75 to $1.00—Wow, then $1.75. I could not look around quickly enough to see where the bids were coming from. There appeared to be two bidders, and I don't remember who the other bidder was, but the second bidder stood in a cluster of Scouts and was still in the bidding.

When I could focus long enough, I saw him raise his hand at $1.75—it was Jamie! Shirley was bouncing at my side, her new glasses sparkled like planets, and my face flamed like a coal in the corner stove. The auctioneer said "Sold for $1.75—to Jamie Roy Mullins."

HE BOUGHT MY PIE! Oh, what will I do now? I don't know how to contain this emotion, and move into this new place. I don't know how. Will we sit together? Will he try to hold my hand? What will I do? Will he still want to be my friend? People get crushes, and then don't speak when they break up. I heard my sister say that. What will I do? What will I do?

I honestly don't recall much of the remainder of the evening, but am sure we set together as we ate butterscotch on paper plates and avoided looking too closely at each other. "His lips are something wondrous fair. The truest eyes and the kindest hands. I love the ground on which he stands." The ballad hummed in my head.

At the close of the evening, everyone trooped down the hill to the corner Esso Station where parents and cars were waiting for those who had come to town from a distance.

I only had to walk to the end of town and cross moonlit bridge with its lacy patterns to get home. For once, David had no teasing remarks, but I was sure they would come later.

I would long remember the pie supper night when black, black, black was the color of my true love's hair. In later years, I included it in concert performances, and as I sang, butterscotch and Jamie floated in and out of my consciousness, and I delivered them to appreciative audiences.

Jamie Roy Mullins

■ First Perm ■

In the week before Easter, my oldest brother, Robert, was home for the spring break. He attended V.P.I. (Virginia Polytechnic Institute), and arrived home looking extremely polished, trim, and full of good advice.

Taking one look at me—5'5" tall, 120 pounds, soon to be thirteen, size 34-B breasts (unencumbered breasts at that), and long pigtails—he conferred, I suppose, with Mother and older sister Frances. It was decided some major alterations were necessary in my appearance: at once!

A trip to the local department store, The Federated, where several sizes and styles of brassieres were brought home. No way would I try them on there, with everyone knowing what was going on. A Maidenform was selected. It had cone shaped cups and starch in the linings. How in the world could I run, move or play in this contraption? I would have to try, because no one would take pity on me.

Next—the hair. What to do with that? My sister had naturally curly hair, so she washed, pin curled, and brushed, and it would cascade to her shoulders in shiny waves.

My hair was a flat-out mess. Thick and straight, with a mind of its own. Pins would jump out. Clasps were constantly askew. Ribbons—forget it! The newest item in hair care was the home perm. Toni was the number one choice, but for some reason we chose Richard Hudnut. (I may be imagining this name, but it comes to mind.)

So it was decided that Frances and her friend Betty Christopher would give me the works Saturday afternoon before Easter Sunday.

I sat on the front porch and someone unceremoniously cut my foot-long pigtails one by one. I felt very exposed, but since my hair was still touching my shoulders, I thought maybe it wouldn't be so bad.

We then moved to the kitchen for washing, reading instructions, laying out equipment: rollers, combs, bowls, towels, snacks, etc.

When the solution was opened my whole head opened with it. What a foul, rotten smell! Sinuses aflame, eyes running, and stomach sending signs of rebellion, they began the hours-long process of "beautifying" Lena's hair. Betty was on one side and Frances on the other. I think they evenly divided it.

The processing time was probably an hour, but they gave it an additional thirty minutes or so to be sure it took. By then my scalp was stinging with little chemical burns.

When the moment of truth arrived—and the rollers were finally pulled, yanked, and unrolled—my hair had taken so well that it ballooned to the size of a bushel basket in a matter of minutes. My hair was good and frizzed. It was also discovered on trying to comb it, that one side had been rolled under and the other side rolled upward. So there was this schizoid, off-balanced look—one side flying, and the other frizzing down. This was pre-Afro, pre-softly tangled curls, pre-conditioners, mousses, gels and other such helpful aids in managing such a mess. The thought of cutting and wasting all that time and money was unheard of, so the perm stayed.

Did I say the odor of the solution, at that time, would linger for weeks, and a fresh do was absolutely overwhelming? The rest of the evening is still a blur. I think I threw up a couple of times, prayed I would wake up with my old hair back, slept alone. Frances couldn't stand the smell, so she slept on the couch.

I woke to an even larger mass of hair. It had doubled again overnight. Everyone avoided me for some strange reason as church time approached. I had a new dress Mother had made, and it was stretched to the nth degree with the new chest size. My hair was slicked down with some of Dad's hair oil. Not exactly slicked down, but it was oiled enough in front to keep it out of my eyes.

Going to Sunday School was agony! What happened to you? Phew, what's that smell? Who's in there? Lena the Hyena? Here comes Frankenstein's bride. As I was scheduled to sing with the Choir at the service and a solo as well, I knew I had to get some control. So chin up and with a "I'll punch you out if I hear another word about my hair," on my lips, I threw out my chest and said, "Don't you guys know anything about the latest styles from Hollywood? I saw this in *Silver Screen.*"

I was truly on the edge of style even in 1949.

*Robert Cantrell, Freshman year at VPI
(Virginia Polytechnic Institute) c1949*

■ ■ ■

*Lena Carol Cantrell
c1947*

■ ■ ■

▪ To Pay a Debt ▪

Before dawn in late November,
nineteen fifty-two,
rain fell as floodgates opened
day after day.
Johnny Ike came to repay a debt
knocking at my father's door.

Mornin Fitzhugh, howya' doin',
A voice squeaked from full-moon hat,
sodden, rippled, and wide.

Come to hep you—hep and pay
what I owes you.
Allers pay—Johnny does.
Come to rake them leaves
you said needed doin'
when you gimme some money
last summer.

Reckon this rains gonna stop?
Show me whur the rakes is
you use to do the job
and I'll commence on it.
Allers pays back, Johnny does.
Don't take somethin' fur nothin'.

No way you can work
in this falling rain.
Dad spoke, amused at his
early morning caller.

Go on home, Johnny, go home
Come back when the snow falls.
Pay me back then.

Knowing as times past
and times to come,
Johnny never struck a lick of work
in his life, that anybody heard tell.
Sly he was in ways and means,
studyin' and figurin' to pay back
folding money,
doled out to "get him by."

Well, I'll be on my way,
but I'll be back for shore.
Johnny pays back, he allers does.

Fore I head off up the road,
have you got a cigarette or two,
maybe dollar, to get me by
till check day on Monday?

I thank you Fitzhugh, I surely do.
Yep, coffee would be fine.
Beings you're at it,
a drab of sugar I like—
and some biscuits
would be mighty nice.

Well, I'll be off, but I'll be back
as shore as moon's gonna shine,
be back when the snow flies.
Johnny allers pays, yep he does.
He allers pays.

▪ Meeting Jim Crow ▪

The summer of '53 I took a job in Richmond, Virginia. Told a fib of high school graduation. Diplomas equaled commissions in retail production. Sister Frances and new brother-in-law James were amused at my rapid transition to city girl.

I was gently trained to sell fine jewelry on the first floor of Miller and Rhodes Department Store. Trafari gold, Majorca pearls, and filigree lockets were perfect for bride-to-be's token gifts.

The senior sales lady with gray chignon and queenly poise looked with distain at this mountain upstart who spoke of rite back, good nite, and so nice. Diamonds paled before the icy glare of her stare.

My heart was joyful and light in June as I rode the Broad Street bus to and fro, skipped in red patent Capezios while black-and-white-checked skirt swished below a red cinch belt. A white eyelet blouse was cool in the late afternoon sun.

The Friday bus was crowded and seats scarce, but I was lost in thought of weekend plans—maybe the beach or try a new hair do.

"Move to the back of the bus." "Keep moving." "Move to the back." I complied and kept moving as workday bodies pressed and touched. I moved and observed it was less crowded. A few waiters, maids, and a soldier or two. All silent and dark.

I saw a space, "May I sit?" She was young like me, but her eyes opened wide and she moved to the window. I do not know how long we sat before I was aware of hostile eyes and buzzing voices focusing toward someone or thing back beyond me—to the rear.

My companion rose in one motion and tried to step over my legs when the bus came to a sudden stop—hot brakes hissing and back doors jolting open. Voices rose in anger.

"What do you think you're doing? . . . what do you think you're doing?" screamed a voice from the crowd as bodies parted and a path was made for the dervish driver who came to a trembling halt.

Spittle hit my face as he screamed from an inflated head gone red. "Whatta you tryin' to do—Sister? Start a race riot? Don't ja know we got laws? Don't ja know no sittin' with n_____s on my bus? Don't ja know nothin? GET OFF MY BUS. GET OFF MY BUS—NOW."

Hands clutched my eyelet shoulders, my purse and packages fell, my companion leaped onto the seat, climbed over the rail and was gone, no backward glance. I was lifted, shoved, and planted on Broad Street as inferno exhaust took my breath away. My hand comforted my turbulent heart as it pounded. "This is wrong. This is wrong. This is wrong," I gasped and comforted my racing heart.

"Explain this to me, if you can, brother-in-law, law student. Show me these laws. Show me this Jim Crow. How can this be? They were nice people, working people, women with white gloves and hats. There was even a soldier. How can this be?"

These laws were clear and everywhere, but their meanings were lost on me until that moment.

Back to school in the fall, where no one wanted to hear what Jim Crow does and how it was wrong in a country like ours that proclaimed "created equal," and "liberty and justice for all." We memorized it and pledged it daily.

From that day on I spoke, I wrote, I marched, I taught, and even cried. This is wrong.

■ Beauty Contest—50's Style ■

The only reason I watched for and tuned into the "Miss Teen USA" pageant was to cheer for Miss Virginia, who had her roots deep in Southwest Virginia, all the way back to Wise County and Pound. Her grandmother was a childhood friend, and probably a cousin through marriage if not through blood. We could check far into the bloodlines, but that was something we didn't spend a lot of time doing. I just assumed I was kin to most people in town, unless their name was one that only had five or less listings in the phone directory.

Anyway, I tuned in to watch these specimens as one from another age, century, generation gap, and what seemed like another planet. These young misses were curled, polished, glossed, and starved to perfection. They danced, pranced, exuded sex appeal with properly lowered lashes, and glowed like dancing jelly beans in pastel minis, tank tops (if they call them that) and bikinis, then slinky, puffed, draped evening wear. They squealed properly at the calling of each winner, and hid their pain behind perfect smiles and wide-lashed eyes.

They all seemed worthy of winning, because how can you judge a clone? Who was the original? The winning question, "What would you do if you were a teenage boy for a day?" really stumped them, as Miss Kentucky replied, "Gee, I don't know, I don't know what boys do and stuff." She was not a finalist.

The next day, while I was in my early a.m. thinking mode, I had a sudden thought as I bent to retrieve the morning paper from the shrubs. Wow—I was that age once, and I was in a beauty contest! Actually, I went from town—on the stage at the Pound Theater contest sponsored by the Lions Club—to the County Fair at Wise to compete for Miss Wise County. The way I got there is another story and is probably the reason I had buried it deeply all these years. I really didn't win anything at the local show, just got asked to fill in for one of the three winners when her parents wouldn't let her go to the fair to compete. The fair had sideshows, carney people, and sometimes men walked around drunk and whistled at the girls. Remember this was early 1950, and I don't think sex was really out in the open very much, just on everyone's minds.

My brother, Robert, was home for summer from V.P.I. Some may have heard of the job he instigated on my hair a few summers previous, a home perm, and knew by now he took a great deal of interest in me. Taught me reading, sports, introduced me to classical music and musicals. He was a natural teacher and I liked to be taught.

In the weeks before the June contest, businesses were being lined up to sponsor different girls. Cheerleaders were usually the first ones to be grabbed up, 'cause each business didn't want to waste their $25 on a loser; they wanted their name listed in the professional booklet used to list the events during the week-long fair. The Miss Wise County contest was held the last Saturday night and brought out the biggest crowds.

I think I was number sixteen in the roster of eighteen and my dad was the sponsor. There big as life was listed F. L. Cantrell, Contract Hauling, as sponsor of Lena Cantrell. You didn't have to be a genius to figure out how I got there. Robert had persuaded Dad to do this. I didn't actually hear the conversation, but am sure it went something like this:

ROBERT: "You know Dad, I've been thinking about the beauty contest, and how the sponsors get their names on the local program, and you, being a founding member of the Lions Club, ought to sponsor someone and promote your business.

DAD: "Everybody in town knows me, knows what I do. They see the trucks go back and forth through town all day long hauling gravel here and yonder. Anyways, all the girls are taken, from what I hear."

ROBERT: "Well, Dad, I was kinda thinkin' Lena might like to do this. You know she's getting older and taking more interest in her appearance— well, sometimes. Since she's been singing with Geneva Lawson, that new girl, she fixes up more. I've seen her looking at *Seventeen* magazine several times."

DAD: "It's gonna take a heap more than looking at a magazine to get her ready for something like that. I know she talks good, sings good, and can keep a body entertained for hours—even looks better now that her hair has growed out from all that permanent business you all did on her a few years back."

ROBERT: "Ha, ha, ha, that was pretty bad, but it looks good now— long and thick, and I have some ideas about that. I don't spend all my time marching at Tech. We get to check out the girls at Radford and Hollins for dances, and lots of those girls have class. I'll help her get ready, practice her walking, and get someone to get the right makeup. I think it would really be good for her—a good thing."

DAD: "What if she don't want to? I know she is a showoff at times, but this is something real different—they judge these girls on being pretty. I don't want her to feel bad. If you think she wants to—talk to your mother—if she says it's OK, then it's OK with me. Hey, you know if she don't want to do it, you'll know real quick."

Walking was the first thing I had to work on. Robert put a book on my head and had me go up and down the sidewalk over and over. That was nothing; the problem was what to do with my hands. I usually had a basketball or book it them, even when we were just sitting around. Robert was full of instructions, like: "Don't cross your arms." "Don't lean on one foot." "Don't put your hands behind you." "No, not hanging stiffly at your side, let them be loose." "No, that's too loose!" "Hold your head up." "Don't look at your feet."

The dress was what really convinced me, I would be a knockout! It was red. Red satin, with off the shoulder ruffle and a hoop in the skirt. My sister, Frances, had brought it home from college. Think she had worn it to some cotillion club dance, and since I was a healthy sized girl, and she was thin, it fit perfectly everywhere except the length. She was off somewhere teaching at a swim camp, and Mother didn't think it should be hemmed— something to do with needle marks on the satin, or the enclosed hoop—so I was fitted out with a pair of really high, platform, gray sling-back pumps. That wasn't really so bad because I had played in high heels on and off with dress-up clothes. At one time, when I was much younger, I would run in them, climb trees, and dribble a basketball on the school grounds in them, when no one was watching. I figured I could manage the shoes. I had to give the dress a little kick in front with each step or stand especially tall to keep from stepping on it.

Contest night finally arrived. My hair was washed and rolled, some pancake makeup applied with wet sponge, red lipstick carefully blotted. All my friends were contestants also, and I thought what a lark, what an absolute lark! They looked fresh and lovely in pastel, puffy tea-length gowns, soft, flat ballerina shoes, sparkling eyes and lots of giggles. When we arrived for a run-through, before the actual event, the coordinator informed me right away, the dress looked a little too old, and I would definitely have to leave my glasses off. Off? Was she crazy? How could I see? How could I get across the stage with no glasses? Oh God! I've had it.

Shirley, one of best friends, wore glasses also, but she was accustomed to taking them off, especially in study hall when we shared tables with some of the better-looking junior boys. A plan was worked out whereby I would hold her glasses when she made her stage walk and she would hold mine.

I don't actually remember very much about the walks across the stage, other than a dark blur when I tried to see past the footlights, and lots of whirling spots when I looked away. Think I walked, kicked out skirt, looked out to see who was there, then took off for the wings. Somehow I made it through two elimination rounds (four at a time), and almost felt like a movie star in off-the-shoulder red.

I was happy, my friend Geneva won first place, a Bolling girl second, and can't for the life of me remember who won third. Whoever she was, her withdrawal from the county competition enabled me, with a last-minute notice, to compete at the county fair. Big-time beauty stuff!

Robert was happy and full of more big ideas, and said with lots of work I might have a chance to place in the county contest. I knew he was nuts at that, but I said, "Hey, we get in the fair free, and we get a book of passes."

Youngest brother, Mickey, was excited at the idea of all the rides for free, and second brother, David, was really strutting around, 'cause he had the worst kinda crush on Geneva, and she talked to him some when she came around to practice our duets. I liked that he was being especially nice to me these days—no teasing about the beauty practice and the lipstick. He loved singing some crazy old song about "Lipstick makeup leave behind, makeup takes up too much timmme," something about then, "going fishing."

I felt almost experienced when we arrived at the fair grounds for an afternoon practice, until I got a look at the girls from Norton, Wise, Big Stone Gap, and Coeburn. Makeup kits, separate bags for hairbrushes. Mothers walking around carrying puffed-out dresses, patting their faces, and telling their daughters, "Honey, just calm down, you are the prettiest one here. If the judges have eyes in their heads at all, I know you will win."

Geneva looked great in her blue, silvery strapless, a knock-out tan, and her swimmer's body. She had poise seldom seen in our area—she had moved from Gary, Indiana. I thought she could win, and then I could be a friend with Miss Wise County. I would definitely settle for that.

The crowds packed the outdoor ring, and focused on the collapsible stage erected in the center, with steps at either end. A curtained waiting area hid the contestants until their name was called.

With head slightly spinning from four rides on the Octopus, eyes misty from the powerful spotlights following me as I crossed, and Robert's final instructions echoing in my brain, I made my entrance, stepping cautiously to avoid cracks in the plank floor that was covered with graveside grass—I slowly made my way across this potential minefield. Don't stumble, look up, look sideways at the crowd, act natural, no squinting—open your eyes wide, move your arms slowly, pivot on left foot (never learned that turn like a model showed us), face crowd, smile wide, pivot on right foot then step off toward home.

A lady sitting behind my family had comments for each contestant as they entered and reentered. Her comments for me were something like this: "Look at that little gal in red. Who does she think she is? Nose in the air, slow walk like a queen. Bet she thinks she's hot stuff!"

On hearing this Robert laughed his loudest and said, "She sure does lady, she sure does."

■ ■ ■

Geneva Lawson became Miss Wise County, and I had a famous friend. Geneva married my uncle, Fred Cantrell, the next year and we did not sing anymore.

▪ Dad ▪

My dad was a bit of a roly-poly, but firm and solid. He loved to eat the food of his childhood—biscuits and gravy (Sunday morning gravy was his specialty), wilted lettuce with hot bacon drippings, mashed potatoes, and pork chops—all the rich comforting foods of the mountains.

His smile was gentle, and seemed to be hovering around his mouth ready to spread at the slightest prompting. Laughter came easily to Dad, and rose from his Santa Claus belly to his face, then danced and lit his warm brown eyes.

Dad was not a disciplinarian in the traditional "spare the rod and spoil the child" sense, that was Mother's specialty. A handpicked switch from the nearest tree was a frequent visitor to my young legs and I danced to its tune. Dad controlled with a look, a sign, or deep hurt shining from unshed tears. We, or rather I, could be subdued and contrite in an instant at a look of disappointment or disapproval at my conduct. This was a rare occurrence, because he was known to be overly proud of his five children, and followed our activities with unhidden pride.

We were the brightest, most athletic, most talented, and generally the best kids in town. He did brag on us so, carrying clippings or pictures in his shirt pocket and pulling them out frequently as he made his rounds. We were well-known on the street, the corner service station, the mines, church, weekly Rook games and everywhere he went. "Stranger" was not in my dad's vocabulary.

His friends and our friends still tell "Fitzhugh" stories after all these years. Stories of fishing trips, political battles, and ways he had helped and encouraged those who he came in contact. Dad was often called a "Softy."

Some lessons of life that I learned from him aren't new or profound in this day of pop psychology and a million self-help books, but Dad lived them, and I imagine he wanted to give us all the tools he could to cope with lives yet to be lived. He was married at nineteen, and had five children by the time he was twenty-nine, became a successful businessman with little education beyond elementary grades, so I reckon his thoughts on life and a philosophy to live by could be needed even today.

1) Pay your own way.
2) Work hard.
3) Be willing to help others—always.
4) Take risks.
5) Save something of every dime you earn.
6) Be ready to play and have fun.
7) Take joy in the company of children.
8) Unconditional love.
9) Treat those with less with sincere respect.
10) Share your life.
11) Laugh.
12) Tears are OK.
13) Women and girls should have the same opportunities as men and boys. Dad was my first "women's libber."

Dad was no saint. I am sure there were shades in his life that were very human and unadmirable. There was a temper (he would bite his tongue or chew on it when angry to keep it under control). He was easily wounded and would hold on to a wrong, indulged in unhealthy practices even after his first heart attack spared him. He knew the need to alter his lifestyle—no smoking, moderate exercise, no salt or rich foods, and remove sources of stress.

His passion to live life fully overcame his will to moderate, even though he tried very hard to follow these new commandments for healthy living. Little things began to creep into the routine. I found the saltshaker in his robe, after a pass around the porch to check on the sun-ripening tomatoes. He persuaded his sisters to fix him hamburgers at their diner, resumed his front row seat at basketball and football games, and paced with the progression of the game. We now had a black-and-white TV with weekly coverage of major boxing events. He loved to sit on the edge of the chair, gaze at the fuzzy gray pictures, react to the roar of the crowds, and take every blow on the chin.

In November, after a fishing trip to Florida with cousin Orby and the Jackson brothers, he came home tanned, filled with fresh fried fish, and tales of the tricks he had played. They had tried to take such good care of him, even to baiting his hooks and rowing him around and giving him a bell to ring when he needed something. That was good for some good tales when they returned. He would ring, call out someone's name and laugh his head off. All tried to get him to rest, take his medication, and slow down.

Upon returning home, he went on an early shopping frenzy for Christmas in November. A new Ford for brother David, a gray mouton coat for me, red snowsuit for first grandchild Amy, TV for sister Frances and husband James (now a law student and a Democrat), shotgun for Mickey, new clothes for Mother, and wonder of all wonders—new clothes for himself. A charcoal gray suit, soft blue shirt, new tie and gray hat with small red feather. He looked so fit and handsome.

Off to Richmond they went, driving the new car loaded with packages for Christmas on Thanksgiving Day. I was attending Westhampton College there, James was in law school, and David was in nearby Fork Union Military Academy where he would be playing in the game that afternoon. Robert was stationed in New Mexico, a lieutenant in the Air Force.

Since I was playing with the University of Richmond marching band, I would remain in Richmond for their game, while the rest of the family journeyed to Fork Union for the day and watched David play. The plan was to gather in the late evening for more visiting and late dinner.

The night before we had eaten together, played with Amy (the cutest, brightest and jolliest grandbaby ever), exclaimed over Dad's tan and his nifty new outfit, and accepted with genuine surprise our extravagant early Christmas gifts. Lots of hugs, kisses, tears and unspoken words, "Why now all this Christmas giving?"

The day was perfect with the clearest of skies, late falling leaves for more color, and well-dressed families united to cheer for their sons. No one was more impressive than David, at 6'2" and around 235 pounds—he was many men's dream of the athlete in his white and blue battle gear.

Dad did his usual following of the game along the sidelines as the ball moved from goal to goal, and all appeared well and safe.

At sometime after halftime, Dad approached Frances and complained of sharp chest pains and numbness in his hand. A young cadet escorted Dad, Mickey, and Frances to a nearby infirmary to wait for a summoned doctor. Mickey was left to keep watch while Frances returned to find Mother. Mickey watched. Dad breathed. Mickey watched the breathing become a rattle then a gasp. He asked for some water. As Mickey helped him to sit, he died on this perfect day, November 12, 1955. Pieces of myself were lost forever.

A good part of my dad lives on, I hope, in all of his children in the ways they have used his legacy. I know I have tried, not always with success, to live with some of his lessons before me. To say yes to life in all its wonder through amazing joys and heart-stopping pains. Hopefully some of this "yes" has been passed to my sons, the children of my siblings and those who follow.

David Cantrell at Fork Union Military Academy
1954

■ Partaking at the Oasis ■
Youth and Adulthood

I see my days of youth through
dusty classroom windows—dreaming.
Labs and rehearsal halls—learning,
Churches inspiring me to sing
toward Rainbow windows,
sing through the sun's rays and pray for
Life to unfold in—
brilliance, happiness, love,
fame, adventure, and wealth.
I was ready to partake.

Scene upon scene flashes by at hurricane speed
life through windows
Steamed by passion's breath.
Windows of hope and joy.
Waving through windows of endless tears
of good-byes,
as cars, buses, trains, ships and jets
carried me over and away from
my mountain views
I found the Oasis of my childhood
Found it and drank deeply.

■ Piecing ■

Mother, with a water-warped hat,
walked in the garden
and touched her flowers
with Jergen's softened hands.
                    You see these brick bungalows
                        scattered throughout the land.
                            Sears bought and built
                    with wide porches and squat columns,
                                    we had one.
I have a cedar chest
Dad gave to Mother in the 1940s,
I think it was after the War,
when "hard times began
to come no more."
                    The chest is filled with a world of color,
                                swatches of our lives,
                        quilts that bloom when unfolded,
                                    everywhere pieces.
Mother's favorite blue dress,
my yellow, checked pinafore with rickrack,
bold red stripes for Grandmother's apron,
that slipped over her head,
tied at the sides.
                    Crayon colors smudged and faded,
                    all found in these feedsack-backed quilts.
                        Every stitch made by hand, so fine,
                            a Princess with a golden needle
                                    might take.
We slept—
warmed by passed-on Love,
beneath the petals.
                        I saw a blue hand-stitched quilt
                        folded in a box, A Flower Garden.
                        There it was, tossed like a rag
                            or faded towel for a dog
                                to snooze and scratch.
Her hands were
graceful, even in Death.

*Mother in the Garden
(Tottie Cantrell)*

*Family on porch at home
Front row: Frances, Mother, Lena
Back row: Robert, David, Mickey*

■ Best Laid Plans ■

A Wedding Tale

In 1964 I had been teaching in Venezuela for three years, and was preparing to wed a geologist I met there. George, my intended, was from the metropolitan area of Hundred, West Virginia, and I from the even larger town of Pound, Virginia. Fate and geography had arranged for us to meet and wed.

Planning a Virginia wedding, at such a long distance, proved to be more daunting than we had anticipated. His elderly parents were not able to travel, while my mother and siblings would probably travel anywhere to see me married off. I was rapidly approaching thirty and had been considered an Old Maid for years by the standards of the Appalachian culture where I was raised.

Mail delivery between the States and San Tomé was more than sporadic, and phone calls were impossible from this isolated oil camp. After months of frustrating correspondence between Mother and me, it became apparent we should get married here where we met and had mutual friends.

The kids at school were so excited when I casually asked, "Would you all like to come to my wedding?" A shouted, "Yes," was heard in the most distant classrooms.

The plan to wed in Venezuela required us to post bans three weeks before the wedding and have a civil ceremony. Religious ceremonies were at the discretion of the couple, so we planned to exchange our vows at the school auditorium-Protestant Church.

I had selected a green-and-white dress for the civil event, and lovely Tai pearl-blue silk for the church wedding. A friend and travel companion for past summers had bought the silk in Bangkok where she had gone on her honeymoon the previous year.

Single teachers seemed destined to marry bachelor engineers or geologists in these isolated camps, a fact I realized shortly after arriving when the "eligibles" casually met the plane bringing in the new group of teachers. We definitely got the once-over, and "get acquainted parties" began immediately.

Once our friends were informed of our plans to marry there, everyone wanted to help and quickly began organizing the event and fiesta to follow. We decided on May 1 for the civil, and June 1 for the Big Day. George would have vacation, and school would be over. A well thought-out plan.

To meet the requirements for a license, we had to go to the nearby village, Tigre, present our passports, visas, proof we did not have other spouses, and two Venezuelans as character witnesses. When George called on Wednesday night, April 18, that all was ready for a trip to Tigre at lunch break the next day, I thought, "Ok, let's do it!"

George picked me up at school. Wrap skirt, sandals, and copy-machine stained hands completed my ensemble as I set off to change the rest of my life.

We were quiet as we left the camp compound, passed through the gates, and drove down the small road that led to Tigre. It was a Technicolor day. Pigs, chickens, and loaded burros were in abundance as we entered the village and found the oficina.

The structure was adobe with dirt floors, khaki-clad officials with pistoles and jokes about our mission. Our witnesses, Polineo and Solarzeno, advised us they would need a few private minutes with the officials and maybe dole out a few bolivers to expedite the paper work. While they spoke in the bright courtyard, we remained in the shadowed room, with its wide, scarred table, thick ledgers stacked, some bougainvillea in a large milk-tin reaching for the sun. I observed the sheen that had appeared on George's usually cool and composed face, took a few quick breaths. "Am I really doing this, getting married?"

The group finally returned from their courtyard conference, all smiles, backslapping, and handshakes for George. Nods and slight leers for me, as they examined our produced documents.

Polineo then explained we would each be asked a question in Spanish.

For George, "Do you wish to marry with this woman?"
He would reply, "Si."

For me, "Do you wish to marry with this man?"
My reply would be, "Si."

They asked. We replied with our Si's.

One of the ledgers was opened, pen dipped into bottled ink, and we signed
our names. George Edward McNicholas—Lena Carol Cantrell.

More handshakes, smiles, backslapping, and sly sideways looks seemed to
fill and echo 'round the room, and George was visibly perspiring. My hands
became damp and developed tremors. The document was presented with a
bow, more handshakes and smiles.

I thought, "If they are so hysterical about a mere application, wonder what
they would do with the real thing? Glad we have that all planned. Advance
invitations, a few flowers, friends, and small party at the local diner and
gathering spot, Chepas. Now back to school and afternoon classes."

Quietly and hesitantly we got into the dusty, faded-blue Volkswagen that
was George's pride and fortune to own. When he handed me the papers to
put away in the folder, I began to read: "Abril 21,1964, Estado Anzaitegui."
"Ah," I thought, "'Certifica de Matrimonio'? that sounds like 'marriage
certificate.'"

"George, what does 'Certifica de Matrimonio' mean?" I mumbled, "Sounds
like and looks like 'marriage certificate' to me, what do you think? Here,
take a look."

He turned off the engine, looked over to see that Solarzeno and Polineo
had not started their car and were looking intently at us with huge
smiles and nods. Polineo held his hand up, crossed them as if they were
shackled.

Meanwhile, George was scanning the paper, turning it this way and that.
Scratching his head, he said, "Looks like some kind of mistake. Let me
check it out."

He motioned to the guys, and they met him at the back of the car. Again,
laughter (from them), backslapping, and a mouth-open, vacant silence
from George. They all looked my way several times, waving the paper and
pointing.

George turned abruptly, returned to the car, saying quietly as he entered, "It seems we are married. Those clowns thought it would be a good joke, to speed everything up, paid a few bolivers to make it official, seems like—um—we are—um—married. What do you think?"

"What do I think? What do I think?" I muttered. "Look at my hands, look at this skirt, look at my dusty shoes! What did they think they were doing? I might have changed my mind. My dress is not finished. How is this possible? Did you know what they were planning?"

One look at his pale face, I knew the answer, he would never have done anything like this and was in the same state of disbelief as I.

Then I began laughing and laughing. "Ok, that's done, I still stay in my house, we move the wedding to May. Do you think we can keep this part a secret? How do you ever tell anyone, Oh, by the way, when we got married, we didn't know it! Brilliant planning! Some wedding tale for the children!"

George E. McNicholas and Lena C. Cantrell Wedding
1964

■ ■ ■

For our sons: Michael, Joseph, and Bruce.
In Memory: George E. McNicholas, 1987

■ Oasis ■
Motherhood

In early years of motherhood
I lived in a country called Venezuela
sat by windows on clear December mornings
rocking by babies—one-by-one.

Rocked, hummed, and gazed
on skies forever blue
flowering tree vines
Bougainvillea, Frangipani
golden-yellow, pinkish-red,
entwined and thriving
here and there.

Gardener and maid
sipped early coffee
strong and black
spoke softly of
Navidad-Noche de Pas
and Bueno

I rocked, hummed, and dreamed
of mountains bare, etched
against gray Appalachian sky,
Cardinals flashing through
holly, hemlock, and pine
feeling sharp winds teasing
my face, watering my eyes
and think,
"First Snow is Coming!"

■ Momma's Lullaby ■

Oh my Baby, Baby, Baby
Oh my Baby mine
Let me hold you, hold you, hold you
Now at your bedtime.

While we're rocking, rocking, rocking
I will hold you tight
While we're rocking, rocking, rocking
Everything's all right.

Let me whisper special secrets
Of the world so far and near
Let us count your toes and fingers
Rosy, chubby, oh so dear.

Momma* loves you, loves you, loves you
Loves you Baby mine
Momma loves you, loves you, loves you
Loves you all the time.

See the moon outside our window
Looking happy in the sky
He will watch you 'till the morning
Wakes you from this lullaby.

Close your eyes now baby darling
Let the Sandman in
Guardian angels gather round
While you sleep again.

Oh my Baby, Baby, Baby
Oh my Baby mine
Momma* loves you, loves you, loves you
Loves you all the time.

* use Daddy, Nana or other

Momma's Lullaby

Music and Lyrics

Oh my Ba- by, Ba- by, Ba- by, Oh my Ba- by mine
While we're rock- ing, rock- ing, rock- ing, I will hold you tight
Mom- ma loves you, loves you, loves you, loves you ba- by mine

Let me hold you, hold you, hold you, now at your bed- time.
While we're rock- ing, rock- ing, rock- ing, I will hold you tight.
Mom- ma loves you, loves you, loves you, loves you all the time.

Let me whis- per spec- ial sec- rets of the world so far and near
See the mo- on out- side our window look- ing hap- py in the sky
Close your eyes now ba- by dar- ling let the sand man in - -

Let us count your toes and fin- gers ro- sy, chub- by, oh so dear.
He will watch you 'til the morn- ing wakes you from this lu- lla- by.
Guar- dian an- gels gath- er round you while you sle- ep a gain. -

Words and music by Lena Cantrell McNicholas,
Charlottesville, Virginia

▪ Sing Along ▪

Music and lyrics beckoned to me when I was young
early teen and more
throw me a kiss from across the room
during some enchanted evening

I sobbed over fair maid Barb'ry Allen
and young love, while roll with me Henry
enticed and throbbed of forbidden pleasures

I dreamed when I was feeling blue,
and thought dreams really do come true,
when you wish upon a star.

Faraway places with strange-sounding names
elicited sighs and produced visions of
seeing pyramids along the Nile and sunsets on tropic isles

I marched to we shall overcome and believed we could
until where have all the flowers gone
pulled at my heart, gut, and soul.

I wanted to scream, pull my hair, and run
to the river and pray—we're gonna study war no more.

▪ M I A ▪

Appalachian Ballad

One clear day in August
Nineteen sixty-nine
A pilot lost, was one of us
And, Oh, he was so fine.

A local boy, this flyer
From over on, The Pound
Was shot down (somewhere)
Flying toward Vietnam.

Most men around these hills
Dig to earn their bread
Scott Dotson looked way beyond
To skies for life instead

"I'll never go into the ground
Ma, I am gonna fly,
See the world from way, way up!
Go soaring 'round the sky."

Chorus:
Could you wear the bracelet?
Would you be so true
to an unknown face—still missing?
For love—of Red, White and Blue?

A mountain girl, called Lisa
sat on the porch and heard,
It's a shame, a real bad shame
Scott Dotson was his name.

She got a silver bracelet
Wore it night and day
Proud to wear for the world to see
Scott Dotson—her M I A.

Memories fade, people forget
men dead, wounded, and lost.
Tempted, teased, and almost bribed
She never took it off

Scott's body was finally found
still strapped to his mighty ship
Jungle vines did cover them
Shot down, on this final trip.

A crisp, cool day in November
Two thousand and two
A woman, Lisa, traveled far
For a burial that was overdue.

In Arlington National Cemetery
Thousands sleep under the moon.
Flags fly crisply, taps sound briskly
While hearts beat sadly in tune.

Lisa stood quietly among the crowd
No notice was taken of her
as she knelt (and) placed—without fear—
A bracelet on the coffin, near.

Chorus:
Could you wear the bracelet?
Would you be so true
to an unknown face—still missing?
For love—of Red, White and Blue?

■ Poem Found in the Family Bible ■

Tottie Baker Cantrell
1912-1997

Once I had a little girl
she didn't have any curls,
but she was the sweetest ever
and to leave me, I thought
She will never.

But all too soon she is grown
and gone and left her mother
All Alone.

I know some day
just wait and see,
She will come sailing back.

And now Heavenly Father,
I leave her in your care.
It is a comfort to know
You are everywhere.

So my dear God,
I humbly Pray,
Bring her safely home
to me.

▪ Bringing Robert Home ▪

July 1983

Over chilled, dry martinis in the brownstone's courtyard in Washington D. C., iced tea on the wide porch of our home in Pound, biscuits at Hardee's in Buena Vista, Robert, my oldest brother, and I had often contemplated returning home to southwest Virginia, starting some vague business that would combine our mutual love of teaching, political action expertise, and passionate desire to make a difference for those who had not had our advantages or experiences beyond the mountains. An unspoken factor, hovering, pulling at our hearts, was very simple—we were homesick.

We often discussed the pros and cons of trying to return to our mountain hometown with the humorous name of Pound. I once received a card from a new friend addressed 16 oz., and it arrived! Could we be effective enough to make a difference? Would the adjustment be possible after years of exposure and stimulation experienced in D.C. and Venezuelan and Nigerian oil compounds, as far away as a planet from these mountains?

▪ ▪ ▪

Vol. 129, No. 97
Washington, Wednesday, July 13, 1983

Congressional Record
Proceedings And Debates Of The 98th
Congress, First Session

A Tribute To The Late Robert Cantrell

(Mr. Jones of Oklahoma asked and was given permission to address the House for 1 minute and to revise and extend his remarks.)

Mr. Jones of Oklahoma. *Mr. Speaker, I take this time to inform my colleagues of the sudden and tragic death of my good friend and a former outstanding public servant in Congress, Robert Cantrell. Robert was killed in a one-car accident last*

Friday morning in southwest Virginia when he was on his way to pickup [sic] one of his children from summer camp. . . .

■ ■ ■

The aging black hearse eased into the narrow space that left it parallel to the low stone wall, but half its length still on the narrow mountain road in front of our home, a 1920s brick bungalow, reported to be the first brick house built for miles around. Oak trees and a massive laurel, a natural sheltering place, shaded a wide porch on front and side with squat, wooden-based brick columns. Those gathered, paused to watch with expectation this latest arrival. A few dents were obvious as road dust settled over the van's ancient wax and dubious shine, yet it spoke "dignity."

I stared stupidly at this intrusion, thinking, "What? What? Who . . . is this?" Cousins and neighbors were speaking in ripples as I stepped from the porch to meet a strange woman as she walked hesitantly 'round the front of the hearse and stood between stone pillars at the end of the shadowed walkway. Holding a rumpled piece of paper, peering over small wire spectacles, she stretched her arm forward as she asked, "Do you know where the Cantrell home is? I am looking for Robert Cantrell's family—we seem to be lost. Can't find the funeral home," her arm vague in its gesturing. "A boy at the station over on the main road directed us this way." How can this be happening? They were supposed to go straight there.

■ ■ ■

Robert Cantrell was one of those priceless public servants without whom this institution could not function.

■ ■ ■

I moved nearer, adjusted my large black-rimmed Corning sunglasses, cleared my throat a couple of times before answering, "Yes, you are at the Cantrell home, but the funeral home is further on, at the edge of town. Stay on this road until you come to the large iron bridge at the edge of town, turn left. No, before that, you turn right at the small bridge, then a quick left onto the main highway—at a really sharp blind curve, you have to be careful, then you go about a mile to the large iron bridge at the edge of town. Then a turn left—there you will see a long, low, stone building, it used to be Pound High School, and we lived beside it for years. Anyway that is the funeral home. It has a sign."

I moved closer to the lady, seeing she was not young, was flushed, rumpled, and confused at the directions I was trying to give. Oh, these are Robert's friends from Buena Vista who own the funeral home—why are they here? They seem so frail—I thought they were sending him with a driver?

■ ■ ■

Robert Cantrell came to Washington in 1961 as a congressional assistant to the Representative from his district in southwest Virginia, Pat Jennings. A few years later, he was appointed Executive Assistant to Mayor Walter Washington. In that position, Robert Cantrell contributed mightily to the successful launching of a renewed experiment in local self-government for the District of Columbia.

Robert completed 20 years of Federal service here on Capitol Hill as an important House committee staff member. Along the way, he was very active in promoting the arts and cultural opportunities of our Nation's Capitol City.

■ ■ ■

I approached the vehicle with apprehension, speaking to the lady and elderly driver at the same time. "Hi, I am Lena, Robert's sister. We met briefly at the service yesterday in Buena Vista, but with all the confusion and so many people, we didn't expect you to bring him. Continue on this road, take the first right across a small bridge, turn left onto the main road, but please be careful. It is on a blind curve, look quickly both ways then straight ahead where another small road enters—that's Bold Camp. Turn left and go straight until you get to the iron bridge I told you about. It is not very far. Do you think you can find it?"

I then saw another older gentleman in the cab. He looked at the driver and the lady as she joined them. Confusion, fatigue, and pain were evident in their voices, as one kept on saying, "We don't usually make these road trips anymore, but we wanted to. We just wanted to. We wanted to bring Robert on home."

■ ■ ■

Following his retirement from Federal service, Robert Cantrell, with his usual gusto, jumped into a new challenge as treasurer and financial manager for Southern Seminary College in Buena Vista, Virginia. Partly, he liked the new challenge. Mostly, I suspect, this opportunity brought him closer to his family home in southwestern Virginia. Whatever the reason, it was obvious that Robert

Cantrell's experience, enthusiasm, and ability to bring diverse people together for common cause, reaped rich dividends for the college and community.

■ ■ ■

Shaken as I was from the past three days, dying inside as I flew alone from Houston, met with Mother, sister Frances, and youngest brother Mickey, I had to keep moving. I flew to Buena Vista on a plane loaned by a local, big-time miner. Sunlight illuminated the ivy-covered chapel as we shared our grief and stories during Rob's farewell from friends there and those who caravanned from Washington. I had returned earlier with his children in preparation for this, his final journey. First to the school, now Sturgill Funeral Home, next to receive friends that night, then services the next morning at Pound Methodist Church, and, finally, leaving him with Dad in Bolling Cemetery overlooking the town.

David, my middle brother, had just arrived an hour before. Finding him had been difficult, as he was off the Outer Banks of North Carolina deep-sea fishing and had been traveling for two days. He was persuaded to take a sleeping pill as an encouragement for Mother to do the same. Both were now sleeping.

I could not give in yet, there was still too much to do—and Mickey was still too dazed to comprehend any of this madness around us. What to do now? These people have come so far, and are so kind. I took an inward grip, and said firmly, "I'll take you—yes, and I'll take you."

The passenger side of the cab opened, and the lady sat down in a small swivel bucket seat. I gasped, realizing there was no space for a fourth person. I could walk, it wasn't far—all the cars were blocked in! The driver, nodded toward the back, and spoke softly, "There's a little seat in back."

■ ■ ■

These are some of the statistics of Robert Cantrell's life. . . . However, Robert had many [sic] other qualities that are not necessarily typical in today's society. He was first and foremost a family man. He was devoted to his wife, Mary, and his children, Charlotte, Fitzhugh, and Robbie. He was a practitioner of devotion to the extended family in the best old-fashioned tradition of American family life. Our family was privileged to be a part of the extended Cantrell family.

■ ■ ■

Robert was there, in the back. How could my legs and body move with my heart tearing and clawing in my chest, shrieks freezing my vocal chords in a painful cramp? One door was opened, and I managed to half sit, half crawl onto the small swing seat in line with the end of the coffin. "I'm alright— you can close it." My knees came to life, bouncing in offbeat rhythms as I smoothed my dress in this instant twilight. The left side of my face was inches from polished mahogany, and I heard the magnolia leaves rustle with each jolt. I refuse to believe you are here. I refuse to believe you are in there. I just won't believe it.

Quietness entered me, and I began to hum, without notes at first then surer as the van swayed and rocked us toward town. Ah, for-se' lui che l'a-ne-ma—Ah, can it be that this is he—La Traviata, one of your favorites—tra-la-la-la—la-la-la-la-la-laaaa.

■ ■ ■

Robert Cantrell had visions and horizons for himself and his family which were considerably larger than the average folk. He expanded the horizons of all who worked with him.

■ ■ ■

"First bridge," I called out directions over the coffin, as we hit a couple of potholes and entered the highway. Sol-lin-ga-ne' tu-mul-ti. "The big bridge is coming up next, turn left down the small lane." Of whom my heart foretold me—how you made gibberish sound like Italian—and how hard it was to learn it for real, to keep a straight face when some of your insane words kept crowding my mind.

"Here we are now—that's where our old house stood. Flood waters took it away. Turn into the lane between the lot and the school. Now follow it to the end."

As the van settled, I was able to lean forward, vocco sotto; this is grand opera, Robert—real grand opera.

■ ■ ■

Robert Cantrell was a generous, exuberant, witty, bright, successful, and dedicated human being whose time on this earth was important for compassionate public policy. In addition, he brought a sparkle to the lives of all who were privileged to be related to him by family ties or friendship.

Other hands were waiting to help unload and wheel him down the wide hall, past the senior homeroom with Miss Qualls of the diagrammed sentence and Shakespeare. Then the junior homeroom, study hall/library with Miss Johnson of the black mark-out pencil for suggestive words and Latin. The Coke nook by the office. Mr. Morris, forever principal in dark three-piece suit, slicked-back black hair and square, rimless glasses.

Spaces with memories as thick as dust motes, reassigned as preparation rooms, coffin storage, viewing rooms and chapel. Faces and voices floated like applause and bravos. Adieu.

Robert Cantrell at Capitol,
Washington, D.C.

Cantrell home in Pound, Virginia

■■■

■ Mother's Eyes ■

Sky blue eyes
gaze at me
Misty blue eyes
entreat me

Who am I?
What's happening?

Please don't leave me.

▪ Legacy ▪

"Mother, Mother! Are you here? Mother, it's me."

I entered our home on the Old Road through the back porch kitchen door. My hair was a mess, my linen pants were more than rumpled, and the blouse was on backward. I dressed with sleepy haste at the early morning call from a neighbor to come and check on Mother. Something was not right.

The drive to Pound from Abingdon took one hour fifteen minutes, and Hardees's coffee did little to settle my nerves and only made me more anxious at what I might find. It burned my mouth, sloshed on my slacks and blouse so much I wanted to scream.

I called again as I dropped my keys on the dining table, licked my burning hands and tossed my purse toward the old easy chair, blue velvet now covering the old worn burgundy mohair.

"Mother! Mo–ther! Please answer me. It's Lena. I just came over for a quick trip and brought Baron along for the ride. He is in the car and wants to get out to see you."

I crossed the living room toward the hall and bath that lead to the bedroom. As I approached the bathroom door, I heard a soft timid knock. I stopped.

"Mother, there you are. Are you locked in? Yes it's me, Lena. Do you need some help? Did you get up too early? Mrs. C. saw you on the porch very early this morning when she was getting her paper. No, no her paper. I know you get up early. I will check to see if the paper is there.

"What? What did you say? No, I don't hear babies crying.
"I don't hear anything. No, Mother, the radio isn't on, I'll check.
"Mother, the radio isn't on, and I don't hear babies crying. No, I really don't hear them.

"What? How many? So many. Oh no. Please don't cry. Don't cry. Just open the door and let me in. Open the door, I will tell you how. Put your hand on the knob. Right in front of you, at your hand. Turn it. There are no babies that need you. No babies. Don't say that, please come out.

"I'll make us some breakfast. We'll have hot oatmeal, real coffee—not decaf. How about some toast and strawberry jam? Just the way you like it. Yes, I'll fix all of it. I know, I know. It's hard to remember how to do all these things.

"I'm sure there are no babies. You want me to check? Ok. No babies in the hall. No babies in the hall or living room. No babies in the dining room. None in the kitchen."

I backed away from the door and moved toward her bedroom calling as I move.

"Now just open the door and we can have some good breakfast.

"The porch? I'll check to be sure. No one is on the porch. I know, you are frightened. I would be too. Of the dark. The light is not on? Can you turn it on? Can you turn the LIGHT ON? The wall. No, it's not gone. The switch is on the wall.

"Come back to the door, Mother. Please listen. Turn the knob and let me in. Your things. What things? Your robe—your gown—your stuff. That's alright. You're wet? Are you wet Mother?

"It will be all right. I'll fix everything. I'll help you dress and get us a good breakfast. I'll help you do everything. I will help you dress and fix breakfast. Ok, I will dress you. It's Ok. I'll give your shoulders a good rub and brush your hair. How does that sound?

"Someone is yelling at you? No, I don't think so. I don't hear it. You are there by yourself and I am just outside the door. Just wait a minute."

I ran to the radio and rapidly scanned the stations until I found NPR and a Chopin etude was playing. I turned it up louder and took a few deep breaths.

"Mother, can you hear the music, listen to the beautiful music. Just listen. The music will make the crying babies go away—the yelling voice will go away. Just listen. That's a good girl. A very good girl. Yes, yes, you are a good girl."

I almost lost it completely as tears gathered, and held in emotions threatened to break forth like a tornado and consume me.

"Yes, I am your Momma, your Momma, and I will take care of you. I will fix your hair, get you dressed. We'll eat and go for a ride. Yes, a ride in the car. A long ride. I know you like to ride. Now everything is quiet, only the pretty music and you can come out of the bathroom. Yes, I can Momma. I can make it all better. I will get you some clothes. Just turn the knob, that's good, just turn the knob—.

"Take your gown and robe and put them on. I will make us some coffee. I won't leave. I'll stay a long time. Yes, I will.

"Here are your things, put them on while I get the coffee ready and find our cups with the gold trim and violets. I know they are our favorites."

I proceeded to the kitchen, straightened my clothing and rubbed my tear-laden eyes as I took the coffee and cups from the cupboard. As the sound of dripping coffee mingled with Chopin, I looked out the window beyond the flower garden at the sun breaking over the mountain.

■ December 23rd, 1987 ■

I remember the crack of grass enclosed in ice
and cold sparkles catching the morning sun
as we walked under the angel-guarded arch
to reach the hillside's newly open ground
almost blood red.

I remember tears too frozen to fall
and the cries of hunting hounds echoing
'round and 'round the valleys and hills
where you searched for arrow heads,
scarlet leaves of *ginseng* and chips of rock
to categorize and store in your handmade
box with the coded lock.

I remember our sons with bowed heads,
fleeting glimpses of the man you were:
the slope of a shoulder, deep blue eyes
beneath perfectly arched brows and sweet
shy smiles: young men—boys in pain

I imagine each mind took its own backward
journey to a time when grass was summer
green and their hearts raced in joyous
rhythms as we arrived each year—
dust puffing like brown, sifted flour when we
eased down the one-car lane that led to
The Farm.

I remember our stunned silence at the final
A-MEN
Our slow walk down the still frozen hillside and
leaving you with the saints who carry your
name in stone: "McNicholas."

Charlottesville, Virginia
December 23, 2007

Bruce, Joseph and Michael McNicholas at the farm in Pennsylvania
July 1971

■ ■ ■

▪ Decisions ▪

The brown bag sits with your golf clubs,
boxes of geology books and once shiny
trophies of firsts, seconds, and thirds.
"Personal Effects" is taped to the side like an afterthought
Your name is neatly printed with bold black marker,
and sharp creases hold it closed.

I moved the bag from the car to hall closet, to laundry room,
to your favorite wingback with striped velvet arms rubbed bare
a tribute to your passion for the Steelers.
Goodwill and Salvation Army know me well,
as young men with strong backs and California tans arrive each week
to cart away remnants of our lives.

As the sun comes to rest atop the rounded, brown hills,
I pour last of the chilled vodka, drop by drop into
an oversized glass with twin olives.
With the first biting sip, I slit the brown bag and pour the contents
onto fresh vacuum tracks of the sandy plush carpet and think of dunes
in an endless desert.

One white, rumpled dress shirt—three center buttons missing—
black and brown reversible belt, blue and maroon striped silk tie—small stain
on one side. I touch my martini-chilled finger to the spot and rub it.
I take from the pockets of a dark grey, pin-striped jacket—size 42 medium—
a parking stub, peppermint breath mints, and a handkerchief still folded.

Matching suit pants were cut from hem to thigh on one leg. They flap
loosely when I hold them by the waist to shake them straight.
Shorts and undershirt are crumpled at the bottom with your favorite black
shoes resoled twice but strangely scuffed at the heels.
Did they drag you into the ambulance?
One black sock.

The martini bites my tongue as I press each item
with trembling hands and fold them as fresh laundry.
What do you do with "personal effects" in brown paper bags?
Garbage bins? Bury? Pack them away in labeled boxes? Burn?
I fold the brown paper bag; spear the last, salty, icy, olive
and carry your "personal effects" to my open suitcase.

Second Reunion

with Cousin George C. ("Patton") Scott—Almost

After days and weeks of entombment during the long, harsh winter of 1995–96, I was ready for anything. I had avoided severe cabin fever by donning layers of warm clothing each day and trudging somewhere. Up and down Valley Street—I would get out! Most days I was the only strolling figure in sight, as the temperatures were in the low double or single digits.

In the course of a conversation with childhood friend and actor, Don Baker, he informed me of his planned trip to the nearby Grundy, Garden Creek, areas to shoot some scenes for a TV movie—yet unnamed. I talked around it and decided to make this hazardous trip, meet him, watch some filming, and attempt to contact famous Cousin George C. Scott. Yes, the Academy Award winner—George C. Scott! His dynamic portrayal of Gen. George Patton is stamped in our collective minds forever.

George had the lead in a coalfield drama and was ensconced in a house in Grundy for the duration of the shoot. All of this I had gleaned from the local newspapers that reported with pride that, "Hollywood Comes to Southwest Virginia."

The "cousin" relationship was due to the fact that his mother and my mother were first cousins. Grandfather Baker and George's grandmother, Martha Helen (Hedy) Baker Slemp, were brother and sister. They were from the dramatic-musical side of the family. Grandfather, described in a local history book as being the best banjo picker in the area, would ride horseback for miles to pick at dances or gatherings, and was a dark, handsome man.

Aunt Hedy was drama personified, with long, black hair (upswept rolls), prominent nose, regal bearing, and the ability to move people to tears with her recitations. She recited poems by Longfellow, Poe, Whitman, and original compositions. As a small child, I saw her tears flow copiously as her voice rose, fell, and carried the listeners through tales of love, death, greed, and her special love of Jesus. Occasionally, she would shout at the local Baptist Church during services or prayers. At Sunday dinner tables, and around the town people would ask, "Did Hedy shout?"

I loved to spend Sunday afternoons with Aunt Hedy, looking and hearing about the beautiful radio-actress daughter, Lena, who had lived in Detroit and died early, leaving behind two children, George and Helen. I would cry with her, when she shared this grief, brush her hair, and bring her a cold cloth for her head as she reclined on her chaise. Pictures were displayed throughout the house, and Lena looked like a movie star with a gloved hand resting on the leather seat of a roadster. Through its open door, posed in black-and-white, her blue eyes were powerful, her face pale and flawless, her smile mysterious.

George and I had met in New York City in the early 1960s at Theatre in the Round, where he and his wife, Colleen Dewhurst, were appearing in O'Neill's "Desire Under the Elms." They were a powerful presence together and gave electrifying performances. During the intermission, I sent a note backstage by an usher, and he returned with a message from George to wait after the performance, and I would be escorted to his dressing room. Pinch! Pinch! This was real New York City and to this mountain girl a moment to store and savor.

We met, chatted, and reviewed bloodlines. George would ask a question with that famous direct, eyes-fixed stare, and then glance away with "umm" when the answer was forthcoming. We had tea. (I had heard that George had a problem with alcohol.) He posed like a brooding Caesar and Colleen smiled that all-encompassing smile; I chattered away. Following what I thought was a pleasant encounter, George escorted me to the street where he placed me in a taxi for my return to the hotel. He wished me a safe journey, thanked me for recalling the family ties to him, and spoke fondly of his time in the mountains.

I was making my way down ice-covered Highway 19 in a four-wheel drive pickup that I had not driven in such conditions—going to see famous Cousin George, far distant Cousin Don Baker, and possibly some moviemaking about the coalmines. Sun sparkled like diamonds on the frozen fields and I sang, "I'm Off to See George Patton." Think "Wizard of Oz" for the tune.

I stepped from the truck onto the thick ice at Garden Creek School, where the base camp was located. Don was there to help me with a ready smile, wire glasses, speckled, grey beard, and red toboggan. We scooted along, talking all the while about the scenes that were being enacted around us.

Not movie scenes, but activity around the line of trailers (for actors), light trucks, miners with blackened faces, police cars, deputies drinking coffee by the commissary trailer, and a lot of movement that was going nowhere that I could see.

After an hour or so watching and milling, we moved into the cafeteria for a hot lunch. The caterers had come from North Carolina and had steaming trays of well-prepared, hearty food for this bitter, cold day. We ate well.

Carryout coffee in hands, we waited outside until Don introduced me to George's personal manager. I explained my mission and connection to the actor. He made some comment that "These cousins just come out of the woods," and gave me a dismissive glance. Undaunted, I gave him my prepared envelope tracing the family relationship, and information explaining I was the namesake of George's deceased mother. Also enclosed in the envelope were pictures of George, Colleen, Mother, and Grandmother taken on a visit to Pound. Mother and Grandmother were presenting George and Colleen with a beautiful, hand-stitched, Lone Star quilt, and all were smiling into the summer sun.

His manager explained that they had finished a difficult inside-mine shot earlier, that George was presently getting cleaned up, would be along shortly and then be off for some shots outside a tipple that had been constructed nearby. Don and I then proceeded to sit on a bench by the door to wait for his arrival. Don was most optimistic and excited at the approaching meeting, and we decided he would explain his connection to the family when he did his scenes with George. Don and I had recently discovered a common great-great-grandfather, so he and George had distant connections. The Bakers were musical and dramatic. Genes do tell, but we laughed at the distant kinship, and Don missing out on the musical talent.

I had some reservations at the outcome of the meeting or that George would see me. Through the years, tales of alcoholism, bad temper, estrangements had circulated through the family, and he might have ceased to regard these southwest Virginia relatives as worthy of consideration. Nevertheless, the note was sent, and we waited. Cold and anxious, we waited.

At last, there was a flurry of activity at the doors; a van pulled close, the motor running; two men with folded arms, stationed themselves on either side. A couple of others appeared at the door with the manager. Momentarily looking away, my eyes returned to see a frail, old man in bib overalls and denim cap. He had pale, sickly skin and ice-clear, blue eyes. He was being led toward us, supported at each side, each step made with caution.

Who was this? Who was this? I moved closer as he approached. Yes, it was George C. Scott. The eyes, chin, and nose identified him as such.

"So you're the girl?"
"Umm . . . Yes, _____," I replied.

George, "Umm . . ."

I spoke again, "We met years ago in New York City when you were in a play there—"

George, impatiently, "Umm . . ."

I tried again. "This is my friend, Don Baker. He has some work on this movie."

George, turning aside, "Umm . . ."

The aide handed me my envelope and moved to direct George toward the van. Slowly, step-by-step he was loaded into the vehicle, settled himself, and proceeded to stare ahead at unseen visions while assistants bustled around, then closed the doors. The van moved forward on glistening ice.

I was momentarily taken aback, and Don was stunned, apologetic and angry. "I can't believe it! I can't believe it!" Don exploded. "He was rude. I feel so bad about this. You would think he would have shown some courtesy."

"Don't worry about it, Don. This day has been interesting, an adventure. We had a great visit, I learned how to drive the truck on slick roads, and saw George, fleetingly. Just don't worry about it. Concentrate on the scenes you have. He probably won't remember."

"Anyway, I'm not surprised. You know Patton was not a courteous man."

"Well, I Tried to See George Patton!"

Cousin George C. Scott
visit to Wise, Virginia
c1961–1962

Lena Slemp Scott
(George C. Scott's mother)

Martha Helen Baker Slemp "Aunt Hedy"
(George C. Scott's grandmother)

Tottie Cantrell, child (unidentified), Evelyn Slemp, George C. Scott,
Venie Baker, and Colleen Dewhurst

▪ Journal Entry ▪

October 10, 1997

Uncle Thurman was buried today on the hill cemetery above town. The day was sunny, crisp, and the mountains radiant with the purest shades of purples, reds, and golds. If I kept my eyes on the hills I could imagine the way it was. Not completely, but in small glimpses. There was the bridge, our house, flowers at the fence, the school, and silver maples turned golden.

I stood at the entrance of the newest funeral home in town of red brick with acres of asphalt. This was my hillside of marching soldiers and swaying dancers. I looked down to the river and the new low cement bridge with thick sides. Swish. Swish. Swish. Cars raced into town. People on foot were nowhere to be found. No latticed patterns of rising steel against the blue sky. My heart felt squeezed. A piece of oversized mining machinery had struck the entrance to the bridge a few years earlier, and the end collapsed into the river. It took days to blowtorch and dismantle it enough to haul it way on flatbed trucks, with New Jersey drivers, to a scrap yard. The driver had misjudged the height. Some said it should have come down long ago. Some were proud of the new modern bridge that monstrous pieces of equipment could pass over to the coalfields.

The white frame house no longer sat beside the schoolyard. The house with the wide, cool porch and apple trees. Our grape arbor swing, smokehouse, and gardens were replaced by a four-stall car wash. Trash barrels overflowed and uncoiled vacuum tubes sprawled where the June apples bloomed and Mother stretched the clothes to dry.

A double-wide, reborn as office space, squatted at the upper part of the garden and the remainder of the lot was filled with trucks, cars, and some rusting equipment.

The thirteen silver maples were sacrificed to asphalt parking spaces when the school became the town hall annex and police station; school yard life, silenced forever.

Mother always said she was glad I was away in Venezuela teaching when the trees were cut. She said that I would have thrown a pure fit. She was right, I would have. It would have been a futile fit, but I would have felt good if I had tried to save them.

The only way I could enter the funeral home with any composure, was to turn my eyes to rest upon the church on the adjoining hill. The white steeple stood steadfast against the blue sky and watched over all these foolish happenings.

The Uninvited Guest

Darkness drapes on strong shoulders;
unwelcome, unbidden, unclaimed
if discovered there.
Go away! Do not stay! Go away!

This darkness wends its way
by unknown trails,
blood cells, damaged sires, or DNA?

On it travels until it finds
a proper host, the unwary one—
where it settles like mist or miasma
with savage barbs and selfish ego
who slash and drain with indiscriminate
greed—the Self.

My mother's eyes reflected its arrival
when the common and beloved
became unwieldy and strange.
It crept and moved as boiling lava
covering and choking her
with its dead gray ash.

This darkness cannot be chased away
with tears, pleas, prayers, or vile curses
that damn God (for his lack of care),
and all the Saints who came before.

Now the son, the baby one, with
heavenly blue eyes—so clear so kind
could not bar the door or keep away
the calling card when it arrived at his door.

He found some weapons almost in time.
His bottles of capsules kept in a line
on a kitchen shelf.

His books and music given away
to those who have not stood
in Darkness way.

Salvation arrived by persistence and
prayers of siblings who survive
but keep a wary eye
for the darkening stranger
to arrive and knock.

My name is Alzheimer's
I am coming in!

For Mickey

▪ Moving On ▪

I traveled by car four hours or more
to catch a train in Charlottesville, Virginia
Adventurous, battered, and bruised from vigilance and loss
Widow status, long-standing
An orphan at Mother's passing.

There a cozy vintage station where Jefferson watches,
from evenly framed spaces, tells of his Glorious Deeds.
No mention of Sally here.

A wheezing engine began the journey in New Orleans,
limped through Dixie,
died in Maryland high over a sparse, gray stream.

Fields of sky-wires sway over oily brown tracks
that stain the sudden floating snow.
I have a longing for pine trees, cedar backyard feeders
tempting feathered Carmen from laden branches.

Dolphin sleek Metroliner rescues all with speed and grace.
Some companions sprout cell phones while other hands poise
then dance over silent keys.
Polonaise or Waltz?
Eyes glaze into fathomless space
flash like NEON, "Do Not Approach."

Are my days of adventures lost forever?

Like lightening bolt—I vow, Not Yet!
New York, bright lights, music, and theater.
My sons will meet me there.

I breathe and sigh as my heart picks up the beat.

Lena C. McNicholas
Charlottesville 2001

▪ Is it Time? ▪

When should I take Mother's picture
from the refrigerator door?
Smiling face on a clear summer day—
easy in a white, wicker rocker.

When should I take her down?
Will I know and say—one day
It is time.
Or will I keep her with me forever
on the door?

▪ The Christening ▪

We christened a baby yesterday
A Christmas Christening
Facing a pyramid of red poinsettias
We crowded into seats marked
Reserved

Twenty or more
Gathered to name this descendant of:
      James Millard-Fitzhugh Lee
      Robert Carl-Fitzhugh Lee II
Cantrell's all.

We came to name this newest
Of the coming generation
We came to meet him
To welcome him and to cuddle him

In too brief time to shower him
With love and infuse him with
Memories of those whose markings
Are clear.

He smiled, yawned, looked knowing
We were there to claim this baby
Charles Fitzhugh Cantrell
      "Charlie"

Lena Cantrell McNicholas
Hampton Sydney, Virginia
December 2001

◾ Last Rites for David ◾

Why did you say it's only indigestion
when you are lying in this sterile cocoon
hooked to life with snaked tubes
and no natural breath?

Why am I thinking of a fishing story?
You fishing at Cherokee Lake in a crazy float
of inflated tire tubes arranged for legs to
dangle beneath the water.

You select the feathered fly or a worm from a musty can.
Sausage-sized fingers delicately secure the bait
to barbs so sharp, a light touch brings scarlet drops.
A nearby fisherman made you howl with laughter
when he stepped into deep water, "How's the fishing?"

Thinking you were waist high and walking—He sank!
I was happy you hit the trail through Smoky Mountain passes.
A cowboy as you rode, sang and cooked from a chuck wagon,
fed your guests from seasoned black skillets
then entertained them with tall tales.

This is what I want to know:
Why was I the one who drove like a banshee
to sit by your bed and decide the what's and when's?
To watch your eyes at half-mast through my fogged lenses
and be amazed at same green from same gene?

Would you reply?
You were the one who would fly down the highway,
bully the doctors, comfort my kids,
make peace with my ex as you tell her it was evil
to damn me to Hell as I lay dying.

You would look at this giant of a brother;
say how handsome and tanned he looks
with a white beard and hair like Kenny Rogers.
You would say, no way to those who refused to

See the truth before them—
keep me hooked to drains and bleeps
for endless days and nights with a stem swollen and useless.

You would send me on my way with a whisper
In my ear: "The Lord is my shepherd. I shall not want,"
as tears glistened on your cheeks then
fell in silent drops on my hospital whites.

You would pray
A-men
And let me go.

▪ Class Reunion 2004 ▪

As we meet again
50 years after
the day we were launched
to unknown places—

What do we bring to
this Occasion
that others have not
brought before?

Faded memories of childhood
friends, broken hearts
mended again and again
for some.

Graying hair—or none
thickening waists
and sagging bodies
Outward signs of time passed
And here we are, Old!

But I say,
Old does not travel
the distance to share the Joy.
To Celebrate what we were,
where we came from,
and what we were to become.

We knew each other before
we met at wooden desks,
Wrote on slate with crumbling chalk
and did our sums.

Our Blood knew what was passed
along by those who
bore and raised us.

Our Blood was fed with mountain mists,
water that sparkled then
splashed from deep wells
and clear springs.

Our Blood was fed with
sweet sunlight corn,
tomatoes hot from the vine.

Wild grass, juicy berries
nuts so rich
Sustained hillside cows
fattened hogs
and scratching chickens.

'Till cupboards, smoke houses
and root cellars
were stacked high
Keeping fierce mountain winds,
piled snow and Hunger at Bay.

We knew this when we met.

Now I long to know and ask,
Where did you go?
What did you do?

When you stepped from
that stage
Rolled sheet in hand
tied with a ribbon.
Stepped from the left-handshake
to face the rest of your Life?

Where did you go?
What did you do?

In Memory and Honor of You—
My Classmates—Pound High School—1954

Lena Cantrell McNicholas
1995

■■■

▪ A Dream of Jamie ▪

He came to me in a dream again
This childhood love that could not be,
returned to ease and comfort me.

We sat by a river broad and wide.
We sat in the shade side by side.

No words were uttered as we sat,
but air shimmering as waves
blended our thoughts and sent replies.

Such calmness I have rarely felt,
we sat and breathed while contentment crept—
surrounding us.

All our sorrows, joys, and woes,
our longings held tight within
were revealed, answered, and satisfied
'till all around was aglow!

Time passed and his arm came to rest
on my shoulder, as we sat.

I cannot recall how long we stayed
a minute or an hour.
I only know as I awoke
I cried. "Wait, Please, Jamie.
Don't go."

Lena Cantrell McNicholas
Charlottesville, Virginia
Dec.18, 2006

Jamie Roy Mullins
1934-2006

▪ Falling in Love ▪

When I was twelve, I fell in Love with
a cowboy tall and brave
He had a swagger, sideways stride, and crooked grin
that made me want to swoon
or cry when he appeared in the Saturday matinee—
John Wayne was his name.

When I was a college girl, singing Bach and show tunes
my heart and body throbbed when a young man from
Mississippi moved as if oil lubricated his every joint.
His lazy smile, midnight hair and eyes, beckoned
"Love Me Tender." I was ready.

Approaching fifty, love struck again
and entered my soul. He was rotund.
His moist, Italian eyes warmed my every pore,
when he opened his arms to cradle me with tones from God or Angels.
I reached heights of purest ecstasy or tears fell in darkest grief.
"O Solo Mio." Pavarotti. Please come back.

At seventy, 007 and I are growing old together.

▪ Alone ▪

Alone is uninterrupted reading
a leisurely bath, an undisturbed
Sunday paper
the toothpaste capped and being
in charge of the remote.

Alone is popcorn and diet coke for supper
sleeping all over the bed
with right number of blankets
driving to an unknown destination
without map or plan.

Alone is no one to discuss the latest book
no one to remind you not to read all night
or stay in the tub too long
doing the crossword puzzle
without "do you know?"

Alone is running out of toothpaste or gas
Cold pizza on Monday morning
a cold bed on winter nights
Alone is the number
One

■ Oasis ■

Senior Years

Now I sit by sunroom windows
watch the seasons pass year by year.
I write, dream, read
and recall with guilt, joy or pain
wonders I have seen
Faces I have loved, loves I have lost.

My babies morphing from boys to men
and I laugh at the memories.

Latin rhythms, arias, symphonies
rock and roll, old ballads, hymns
a show tune now and then
comfort me, lull me or
cause me to rise and move to the beat.

Cardinals nest in the holly
squirrels dance with quirky abandonment
as they watch from the knarled oak
this creature acting out as she
Waits for the Sunset.

Lena Cantrell McNicholas
Seattle 2008

▪ Epilogue ▪

To you, my new reader, thank you for selecting my book. I hope it met your expectations and took you to the place of your own precious memories. I have a sequel planned that relates to my life after leaving the Appalachian Mountains. The stories, poems, letters, and essays will cover travels and life lived in Europe, South America, Africa, and maybe Texas. I hope to see you again.

Lena Cantrell McNicholas

▪ ▪ ▪

Another Farewell

Michael (Mickey) Lee Cantrell
1939–2010

On May 24, 2010, as Mickey and I sat in my car watching evening descend over the mountains in Charlottesville, Virginia, he passed away of a massive heart attack after a long battle with Alzheimer's disease.

Mickey's devotion to family and friends was unequalled and those who knew him always recalled his kindness and cheerfulness. Even with the burden of Alzheimer's, he remained pleasant, cheerful and kind. His sense of humor never left him and he loved to say something quirky then laugh and say "that's a joke."

Grateful for having this sweet, loving brother.

Lena

■ About the Author ■

Lena Cantrell McNicholas

As an award-winning poet—reading, writing and performing have been vital parts of Lena's life as long as she can remember. Born in Pound, Virginia (Wise County), Lena graduated from Radford College with a BA in social studies and minor in English. She taught in Virginia, Kentucky, and Maryland before going to Venezuela to teach. Lena met and married George McNicholas in Venezuela; they had three sons and later moved to Lagos, Nigeria. Lena experienced life outside of the U.S. for 15 years.

Lena's writing includes poetry, memoirs, essays, short stories and vignettes. She has been published in: *Appalachian Heritage, Coalfield Progress, Abingdon Virginian, Bristol Herald Courier, Appalachian Women's Journal, Clinch Mountain Review, Wind-The Hindman Edition, The Blue Ridge Anthology 2009,* and *Appalachian Anthology: Silas House Edition 2010.*

Lena McNicholas has received numerous awards for her original work and was Poet of the Month for *A Magazine December.* She is an active member of the Appalachian Poets and Writers, the Blue Ridge Chapter of the Virginia Writers Club, Inc., and the Poetry Society of Virginia.

Life had many unusual turns and journeys for Lena before finding herself widowed and drawn back to her mountain roots. Here she began the new adventure of writing as a way of reliving the many joys and sorrows in her life.

Lena finds contentment in sharing her stories, and receiving joy when others connect to her writings. Now living in Charlottesville, Virginia, *Patchwork* is Lena's first published collection of her poems and stories.

About the Cover

Mountain Mural by Lois Bartlett Tracy

Lois Bartlett Tracy was an established artist in Florida and New York, with studies in Paris, and author of *Painting Principles and Practices* (1965). When she first visited Wise County in the 1950s, she found the mountains there "the perfect country for an artist" and became the first Artist in Residence at Clinch Valley College from 1955–1960. Today, Clinch Valley College is the University of Virginia-Wise. She spent over fifteen years in the mountains as a prolific painter, a teacher at the college at the Inn in Wise, and also taught University of Virginia extension classes in surrounding mountain towns.

"I love Wise," Lois told newspapers and interviewers on the occasion of her return to an exhibit of her work in the Harris Gallery in 1990, "but it is not enough to love a place, you have to feel it."

She and her husband, Harry, "an artist in everything involving food and growing things," filled the Inn at Wise with antiques, paintings by Old Masters, and Venetian glass chandeliers. He built a studio for her on the top floor of the inn with a skylight. A reporter observed that the Inn was like an art colony, with Mrs. Tracy's visiting artist friends from Florida and New York assisting her with summer art classes.

Paintings from her mountain period that hang in offices and private homes are of local scenes. "There was always something saying 'Paint me,'" Lois said, "houses and yards near coke ovens or strip mines, apple trees, fighting cocks in pens, busy little angular birds under trees, the interior of Beatys' store."

"Mountain Mural" has hung in the office of Rep. Pat Jennings; the home of Robert Cantrell in Washington, D.C.; the Southern Seminary College (now Southern Virginia University) in Buena Vista, Virginia.; the home of "Mickey" Cantrell in Rocky Mount, Virginia; and now hangs in the mountains at the University of Virginia-Wise. It was given as a gift to the college by Mickey to honor his parents, Fitzhugh and Tottie Cantrell, and his siblings: Frances, Robert, David and Lena.

Lois Bartlett Tracy remained productive until her death at 106 in the mountains of North Carolina.

CPSIA information can be obtained at www.ICGtesting.com
Printed in the USA
LVOW051417280712

291961LV00001BA/1/P